THE 1800s

A Century of Extreme Drought and Intense Cold

By
HARLOW A. HYDE
DeLand, Florida

"Lord God of hosts, be with us yet,
Lest we forget—lest we forget!

RUDYARD KIPLING, *Recessional*, 1897

THE 1800S: A CENTURY OF EXTREME DROUGHT AND INTENSE COLD

1210 SW 23rd PL • Ocala, FL 34471 • Phone 352-622-1825
Website: www.atlantic-pub.com • Email: sales@atlantic-pub.com
SAN Number: 268-1250

Library of Congress Control Number: 2025916103

PROJECT MANAGER: Crystal Edwards
INTERIOR LAYOUT AND JACKET DESIGN: Nicole Sturk

About the Cover

The photo on the cover is from the Minnesota Historical Society and is a famous photo of a snow blockade from March 29, 1881 somewhere in south Minnesota. During January, March, and April of 1881, the Great Plains region received large amounts of snowfall. At times, the snow was higher than the locomotives and trains could not pass sometimes for days at time. The particular railroad in this photo is the Chicago, Milwaukee and Saint Paul Railway.

Table of Contents

Preface • vii

Part I—Precipitation • 1

Part II—Temperature • 31

Notes on Sources • 111

About the Author • 121

Preface

The climate of North America was significantly different in the 1800s from what has been witnessed since 1900. During the 19th century, the United States and Canada were much colder and drier than during the past 125 years. These two important facts are seldom mentioned today. Indeed, they seem to be studiously ignored in the ongoing debate and discussion concerning the *perils* of climate change. But to understand and appreciate what is happening to the climate in the 21st century, a thorough understanding of what climate conditions were in the past must become part of our common knowledge.

This study will document both precipitation and temperature in the 1800s, using published sources that have been accepted as authoritative. While nearly all the publicity about the climate today centers on temperature, for much of North America, the most critical factor is precipitation. This analysis will be divided into two parts: Precipitation and Temperature. It will begin with Precipitation, to ensure it receives the attention it deserves.

PART I

Precipitation

Annual precipitation totals have been published for all 48 of the contiguous states, beginning with the year 1886. In addition, amounts are available for a few states for one or more years prior to 1886. Although only fourteen years in the 1800s (1886 through 1899) are part of the official record for all 48 states, even this brief period suffices to prove that drought in the 1800s was much worse than anything the country has seen since 1900. The Pulitzer Prize-winning author Wallace Stegner related what he called the Great Drought in his landmark history of the West entitled *Beyond the Hundredth Meridian*. In the section, "Disaster on the Great Plains" (Stegner 1953, 294–304), Stegner calls the drought an "Act of God" and a "slow starvation for water," as well as a "full decade of drought." According to Stegner, "half the population of western Kansas moved out between 1888 and 1892" and "large portions of the plains were virtually depopulated." As evidence of the conditions that caused mass bankruptcies and migrations, precipitation records of the states affected by the drought are presented below, beginning with those with the greatest precipitation shortage.

First, to provide a brief frame of reference, a few basic facts about precipitation are in order. Precipitation has averaged 30.09 inches per year in the contiguous United States (CONUS) 1895 through 2024, 130 years.

Precipitation has increased substantially during this time at a rate of 1.73 inches per century. The least amount of precipitation was in 1910, with 24.90 inches and in 1917, with 25.34 inches. The greatest precipitation in any year was 34.94 inches in 1973, followed closely by 2019, with 34.82 inches. The six driest years were in 1963 and earlier. Conversely, the six wettest years were all 1973 and after. Three of the five were in the most recent completed decade (2015, 2018, and 2019).

Second, at the outset, it must be clearly stated that there is a clear and un-deniable relationship between temperature and precipitation; *cold means dry and warm means wet*. In the past 130 years, the coldest was 1917, when precipitation totaled 25.34 inches. The warmest year was 2024, its precipitation totaled 31.62 inches. The coldest ten years averaged 29.29 inches, while the warmest ten averaged 31.15 inches. This basic contrast holds up no matter the years compared. The high correlation between warming and increased precipitation has been a carefully kept secret of climate change.

Nevada is the driest state, averaging 10.20 inches per year since 1895, fol-lowed by Arizona, which averages 12.23 inches. Louisiana precipitation is the greatest, averaging 57.23 inches over the past 130 years, followed by Mississippi and Alabama with nearly identical averages of 55.91 and 55.42 inches, respectively. Even the remarkable differences between the annual averages of Nevada and Louisiana do not fully reveal the great extent precipitation varies in the roughly three million square miles of the lower 48 states. As discussed later, the nation is further divided into 344 climate divisions, with each state assigned from one to ten divisions.

Many climate divisions in the southwestern states average less than ten inches per year. Arizona Climate Division 5 (Southwest, 10,015 square miles) averages 5.19 inches per year and in 1956 only 0.87 inches of precipitation fell—during a leap year, no less. At the opposite end of the spectrum, several climate divisions in the southeastern states average over sixty inches per year. The basic rule of thumb is that successful dryland farming (with no irrigation) in the American West is extremely difficult in areas averaging less than 20 inches of precipitation per year.

This summary is based on data for the 130-year period 1895 through 2024. But as stated above, the government has published annual precipitation data for each state for all years, beginning with 1886. However, climate division data was not published prior to 1895.

Before proceeding further, it must also be understood that *drought* is relative to the normal amount of precipitation an area receives. Several eastern states experienced record drought in 1930. For example, Virginia's total in 1930 was 24.74 inches. This total was 3.2245 standard deviation (SD) below the mean and therefore qualifies as extreme drought. Virginia's next lowest annual totals since 1886 were 31.15 inches in 1941 and 32.70 inches in 1965. So Virginia's 1930 amount was, in a relative sense, a drought of near biblical proportions. In contrast, Utah's *highest* precipitation total in the 139 years 1886 through 2024 was 20.33 inches in 1941. Twenty-four inches in a year would be unthinkably high in Utah, but in Virginia, this amount was the most extreme drought on record. We must consider what constitutes normal amounts received by each state when considering in the following accounts of drought in the late 1800s.

An Examination of the Drought Experienced by Each State in the 1800s

ARIZONA
113,909 square miles
5th largest in the CONUS
Average annual precipitation 12.23 inches.

Arizona's great drought began in 1886 and did not end until 1905. During those nineteen years, Arizona averaged only 10.45 inches per year. The most intense drought was near the end of this period. For six consecutive years, starting in 1899, Arizona received less than ten inches. The lowest was 7.56 inches in 1899 and the highest in 1901 was 9.22 inches. Perhaps, in a relative sense, the nineteen-year megadrought in Arizona was the most extreme drought endured by any state since comprehensive records began in 1886.

MONTANA
145,522 square miles
3rd largest in the CONUS
Average annual precipitation 18.68 inches

From 1886 to 1895, Montana experienced record drought. The drought was severe with the worst years being 1889 with only 8.94 inches and 1890 with 9.86 inches of precipitation. These are the only two years in Montana when precipitation totaled less than ten inches. Since 1895, 12.62 inches in 1931 was the least amount of precipitation to fall in a single year in the state. In the great drought of 1886, which lasted until 1895, Montana averaged only 14.17 inches. By comparison, the driest decade in Montana since was 1928–1937 when precipitation averaged 16.00 inches.

The oldest precipitation records in Montana are from Fairfield (Fort Shaw) in Teton County, beginning with October 1867. Precipitation in the final four months of 1867, October through December, totaled a minuscule 0.92 inch. The year 1868, the first full year of records, was also very dry, totaling 10.04 inches. But then a drought of apocalyptic proportions began in 1869 and running through 1875, precipitation averaged only 6.41 inches. It ranged from 8.32 inches in 1870 down to just 4.24 inches in 1874, the only year in Fairfield's history with less than five inches. In the first four months of 1876, it appeared the megadrought was going to continue as precipitation totaled a microscopic 0.66 inch. Then finally, in May 1876, Fairfield received a record high 7.19-inch deluge and temporarily the megadrought was over. Fairfield's precipitation in 1876 totaled 14.62 inches. However, the respite was short-lived. In 1877, extreme drought returned with only 8.47 inches. Fairfield's early records add credence to the idea that precipitation declines as we go back further into the 19th century. I challenge those who would deny this to present any evidence they may have.

WYOMING
97,101 square miles
8th largest in the CONUS
Average annual precipitation 15.84 inches

Wyoming also experienced record drought from 1886 to 1895, when the average precipitation was only 12.55 inches. Like Montana, during that period Wyoming recorded two years when precipitation totaled less than ten inches, with 9.79 inches in 1886 and 8.02 inches in 1887. Since 1895, Wyoming's driest year was 2012, with 10.96 inches. Wyoming's driest decade since 1895 was 1931–1940, which averaged 14.57 inches.

COLORADO
103,717 square miles
7th largest in the CONUS
Average annual precipitation 17.97 inches

Colorado's record drought in the late 1800s mimicked Utah's in that it covered the same eleven years, 1886 through 1896. During which, precipitation averaged 15.26 inches. Those who have lived through extended periods of drought know that within multi-year dry periods there are often brief periods of above average precipitation. From 1886 to 1896, Colorado recorded two years of above average precipitation, 1891 with 19.88 inches and 1895 with 19.62 inches. However, Colorado saw four consecutive years, which can only be described as a megadrought, 1888–1891, which averaged only 12.98 inches per year. Since 1896, Colorado's driest decade was 1930 through 1939, which averaged 16.36 inches.

As seen in other western states, after one wet year, 1897, with 21.66 inches, drought returned to Colorado. The next seven years, 1898 through 1904, were all parched, averaging 16.16 inches. To summarize, from 1886 through 1904 Colorado had 16 years of drought, two years of slightly above average precipitation, and one unusually wet year. From 1886 through 1904, the state's precipitation averaged 15.93 inches, much less than in any similar period since.

UTAH
82,144 square miles
11th largest in the CONUS
Average annual precipitation 13.40 inches

Like other western states, Utah experienced record drought beginning in 1886, however, unlike Wyoming and Montana, the drought lasted until 1896, eleven years. During that time, Utah's precipitation averaged only

10.54 inches and included three consecutive years when precipitation totaled less than ten inches: 1886 with 9.67 inches, 1887 with 6.35 inches (the lowest on record) and 1888 with 8.83 inches. The driest year in Utah since 1896 was 2020, which totaled 7.24 inches and the driest decade since the 1800s was 1953 through 1962 when precipitation averaged 11.54 inches.

In Utah, 1897 (16.15 inches) proved to be only a temporary respite from extreme drought. Drought returned in 1898 with a vengeance with only 11.28 inches. The following six years, 1899–1904, brought severe drought. A comprehensive account of the period from 1886 through 1904 illustrates it best. During these nineteen years, the state experienced 18 years of drought and only one year of above average precipitation. The annual average received in Utah from 1886 through 1904 was 11.08 inches. As in Arizona and Colorado, Utah's great drought of the late 1800s continued well into the early years of the 20th century. This forgotten fact is an essential part of our climate's history.

IDAHO
82,747 square miles
10th largest in the CONUS
Average annual precipitation 23.67 inches

Idaho recorded ten years of unrelenting drought in the decade 1886 through 1895. Like Montana to the east, the driest year ever seen in Idaho was 1889, which totaled only 14.76 inches in precipitation. Since 1895, Idaho's driest year was 1935 with 16.17 inches. Four of the ten years qualify as a true megadrought, 1886 through 1889 with an average of only 15.98 inches, even less than in 1935.

Precipitation records for Boise begin in February 1864. Boise's total precipitation in 1868 was only 6.69 inches and in 1885 it was only 12.56 inches. This is pertinent to Idaho's megadrought of 1886 through 1889, because it shows that Idaho's drought probably began a year earlier in 1885.

OKLAHOMA
68,667 square miles
18th largest in the CONUS
Average annual precipitation 33.99 inches

Oklahoma had the most severe drought in its history in the eleven years from 1886 through 1896. During this period, precipitation averaged 28.57 inches. Since 1900, the lowest average for ten years in Oklahoma was 29.94 inches from 1947 through 1956. Oklahoma was the center of the Dust Bowl during the 1930s. However, even during this extraordinarily dry decade, its average precipitation was 30.18 inches from 1930 to 1939. A hot state like Oklahoma is prone to drought; a year when precipitation is 10 percent below normal can be devastating.

In the early 1800s, what is now Oklahoma was called Indian Territory. There are very few climate records from this period, except for one very important set; precipitation records for Fort Gibson, in what is now Muskogee County. These records begin in July 1836. This monthly and annual data was published in the Weather Bureau's *Bulletin W: Volume 2* in 1933, giving the precipitation for Fort Gibson from inception through December 1930. Some years are missing, but plenty are available to show a precipitation trend. Precipitation for the entire period of record in Fort Gibson averaged 38.13 inches per year. But the annual precipitation for the years in the 1800s was only 35.15 inches, while the average precipitation for the years since 1900 was much higher at 40.76 inches. The eight years with the least precipitation were all in the 1800s, with only 18.84 inches received in 1838. The second and third driest years were consecutive. These were 20.21 inches in 1887 and 23.13 inches in 1888. The fourth driest was 1847, with 24.10 inches. In contrast, the years of highest annual precipitation were in the 1900s—59.31 inches in 1908 and 56.96 inches in 1915. Muskogee County is within Oklahoma's Climate Division 6 (East Central) and precipitation amounts are available beginning in 1895. The least annual precipitation in that climate division since

1895 was 23.49 inches in 1963, the second driest was 1936 with 25.12 inches. The remaining 128 years through 2024 all received over 27.50 inches. Fort Gibson's data clearly shows a declining trend of precipitation, at least in Oklahoma, extending back to the late 1830s.

The above brief but perhaps tiresome summary of the data from these seven states suffices to show that drought in the 1800s was much worse than any seen since 1900. These seven adjacent states, totaling 693,837 square miles, had decade-long great droughts within the same ten, eleven, or in three cases, nineteen-year periods. The severity of these dry decades (or longer) far exceeded anything recorded in North America since.

However, this is just the beginning. We will now examine the states where the drought in the late 1800s was more complex, but not necessarily less severe.

NEVADA
110,540 square miles
6th largest in the CONUS
Average annual precipitation 10.20 inches

Nevada is the driest of the 48 contiguous states; severe drought is the norm. In only three years since 1886, has Nevada received over 16.0 inches of precipitation. The highest was in 1983 with 17.80 inches. During the period 1886 through 1895, Nevada averaged 10.06 inches, just slightly less than its normal 10.20 inches. It is notable that during the ten years in question, Nevada experienced the worst megadrought of any state on record. In the three years 1886 through 1888 precipitation averaged 6.80 inches, including the year 1887, which totaled only 5.21 inches, the least ever recorded by any state. Admittedly, since 1895, Nevada has had episodes of much greater drought. The driest decade was 1953 through 1962, which averaged only 8.60 inches. This was the same ten years as Utah, 1953 to 1962, and was the driest decade since 1900.

IOWA
55,869 square miles
22nd largest in the CONUS.
Annual average precipitation 32.56 inches

Iowa experienced the driest decade in its recorded history from 1886 through 1895 when precipitation averaged 28.22 inches. Since 1900, Iowa has had two additional long dry periods: 1930 through 1939, which averaged 29.00 inches, and 1948 through 1958, which averaged 29.22 inches. In Iowa, any year with less than 30 inches is considered unusually dry and any year with less than 25 inches is classified as extreme drought. In the last 139 years, Iowa recorded less than 25 inches only twelve times. Three of these extremely dry years occurred in the dry decade 1886 through 1895.

ILLINOIS
55,842 square miles
23rd largest in the CONUS

As in Iowa, Illinois also recorded the driest decade on record from 1886 through 1895 when precipitation averaged 34.02 inches. The driest decade in Illinois since 1900 was from 1930 through 1939, which averaged 35.25 inches. Since 1972, Illinois precipitation has increased, averaging over 40 inches per year.

As we will see, it was also abnormally dry in states further east.

OHIO
41, 222 square miles

Ohio averaged 36.86 inches in the decade 1886 through 1895 compared to its long-term average of 38.92 inches. The years 1894 and 1895 were the driest two consecutive years on record for the state, averaging only 29.01 inches.

INDIANA
56,290 square miles

Indiana had a similar shortage of precipitation during this decade. The driest two years in Indiana's history were also 1894 and 1895, which averaged 31.32 inches. While it cannot be called a decade of *major* drought in Indiana and Ohio, their data are further evidence of how far east the Great Drought of the late 1800s reached.

OREGON and WASHINGTON
96,981 and 68,192 square miles

Both Oregon and Washington recorded unusually dry decades in the late 1800s. Oregon's driest period was 1889 through 1898, during which precipitation averaged 29.77 inches per year. Oregon's average annual precipitation is 32.03 inches. Washington's driest period was 1886 through 1895, which averaged 38.89 inches, compared to Washington's annual average of 42.26 inches. Neither states' dry ten-year periods in the late 1800s qualify as severe drought. Oregon's lowest decade since 1900 was 1927 through 1936, which averaged 27.71 inches. Washington's driest decade since 1900 was 1922 through 1931, with an average of 36.05 inches.

NEBRASKA
76,872 square miles
14th largest in the CONUS
Annual average precipitation 22.77 inches

Nebraska's overall precipitation averages do not tell the entire story. During the decade 1886 through 1895, precipitation in Nebraska averaged 21.04 inches. This might seem like a minor shortfall given the normal annual total of 22.77 inches. I lived in Nebraska for over 30 years and followed its weather and climate closely. Agriculture in Nebraska is very sensitive to drought. Even a year with precipitation 10 percent less than normal can cause serious problems. Any year with less than 20 inches of precipitation has very adverse consequences. In the seven years 1886 through 1892, precipitation in Nebraska was adequate. There was one extremely dry year with the other six years normal or even above. Then, in 1893, precipitation totaled only 15.87 inches with disastrous results. 1894 saw even less precipitation, only 13.93 inches. These two years averaged only 14.90 inches, by far the driest ever recorded. Since 1900 the two driest years, 1936 and 1937, averaged 16.09 inches. In 1895, precipitation was slightly higher at 18.95 inches, not enough to make up for the dry years of 1893 and 1894. Crops failed for a third year.

KANSAS
82,264 square miles
12th largest in the CONUS
Annual average precipitation 27.24 inches

Kansas precipitation averaged 25.10 inches in the decade 1886 through 1895. While less than normal, for most of the state, this was not a severe drought. However, as recounted by Stegner (p. 409), the drought was devastating in western Kansas (33 counties, 27,689 square miles). In 1890, precipitation in the western division totaled only 13.19 inches.

The following year was unusually wet. But then the next three years were by far the driest in the area's history. First, 1892 totaled 18.70 inches. Then the rains virtually stopped for two years. The total in 1893 was 11.93 inches. Throughout 1894, the extreme drought continued with only 12.19 inches. By 1895, the rural economy had collapsed and many inhabitants simply deserted the land. The census is the best proof of this. In 1890, Wallace County in western Kansas had a population of 2,468. In 1900, following the great drought, its population fell to 1,178, a decline of 52.3 percent. Grant County's population in 1890 was 1,308, but fell to 422 in the 1900 census, a decline of 67.7 percent. Stanton County totaled 1,031 in the 1890 census. In 1900, its population was only 327, down by 68.3 percent. Garfield County's population was 881 in the 1890 census. However, in 1893, its government shut down completely, and it was later absorbed by Finney County. The fact is undeniable—the great drought of the late 1800s was a calamity in western Kansas, and many other parts of the West, far exceeding anything seen since 1900.

NORTH DAKOTA
70,698 square miles
16th largest in the CONUS
Annual average precipitation 17.53 inches

During the decade 1886 through 1895, North Dakota averaged 16.52 inches, which, although less than normal, was not a severe drought. However, the last three years of the period, 1893 through 1895, were all very dry, with an average of 15.70 inches, respectively. Since 1900, North Dakota experienced an eleven-year megadrought from 1929 through 1939. Its precipitation averaged only 14.62 inches.

MINNESOTA
84,068 square miles
11th largest in the CONUS
Annual average precipitation 26.42 inches

Minnesota's precipitation averaged 24.05 inches from 1886 through 1895. This amount was 2.37 inches per year below normal and would be classified as moderate drought. Minnesota's driest decade since 1900 was 1927 to 1936, during which precipitation averaged 22.41 inches.

WISCONSIN
54,310 square miles
24th largest in the CONUS

Wisconsin was unusually dry in the 13-year period, 1886 through 1898, when precipitation averaged 29.70 inches. This is the only such period in Wisconsin, which averaged less than 30 inches per year. It was also unusually dry in Michigan from 1886 through 1895, averaging 30.37 inches.

ALABAMA and MISSISSIPPI
51,609 and 47,716 square miles
Annual averages 55.42 and 55.91 inches respectively

The late 1800s saw the driest periods on record in these two states. In Alabama, in the 11 years 1889 through 1899, precipitation averaged 49.33 inches. Mississippi saw a longer dry period of 13 years. From 1887 through 1899, precipitation averaged 49.49 inches. This was the driest period of ten or more years in either state. Was this a major drought? No, but it is additional evidence that precipitation in the 1800s was much less than received since 1900.

ARKANSAS
53,104 square miles
26th largest in the CONUS
Annual average 50.13 inches

From 1886 through 1904, Arkansas was unusually dry, averaging 46.44 inches. Conway, AR received only 26.80 inches and Fort Smith, AR 31.61 inches in 1885. Therefore, the 20 years 1885 through 1904 were the driest period in the state. Substantial records back this. Since 1904, all periods of 20 years or longer in Arkansas have averaged well over 47 inches.

Precipitation records for Fort Smith, Arkansas, begin in 1882. The five driest years in Fort Smith were all prior to 1940. These include:

- 1917—19.80 inches
- 1901—22.77 inches
- 1936—24.74 inches
- 1910—25.39 inches
- 1896—25.70 inches

In fact, the record drought of 1917 lasted for an incredible 21 months. It began in July 1916, when precipitation totaled only 0.34 inches and continued through March 1918. Since 1940, the lowest annual total in Fort Smith was 26.46 inches in 1980. Today, of course, any droughts even remotely resembling those seen prior to 1940 would automatically be blamed on climate change. No logic or science would support this claim, but it would happen.

KENTUCKY and TENNESSEE
40,395 and 42,244 square miles

As in Arkansas, precipitation was much below normal in Kentucky and Tennessee during the decade 1886 through 1895. Annual precipitation averaged 4.37 inches below normal in Kentucky and 3.57 inches below normal in Tennessee. Precipitation in both states remained far below normal through 1904. The 19-year period 1886 through 1904 constitutes the driest such period on record in Kentucky. In Tennessee, the period 1925 through 1943 received less precipitation than 1886 through 1904.

SOUTH DAKOTA
75,844 square miles
15th largest in the CONUS
Annual average precipitation 19.32 inches

I was born in South Dakota in 1947. My ancestors, on both sides, moved from Pike and Adams Counties in Illinois to the Dakota Territory in 1886 and 1887. The Howards and Spencers on my mother's side included a large clan of siblings and their numerous children. The best land in eastern Dakota had already been occupied, so the Hydes, Howards and Spencers filed their claims and settled in Hughes, Sully, and Potter counties in what is now central South Dakota. But they did not know what they were facing. For the first ten or more years, even their survival was uncertain. Thriving and prosperity were illusions, at best only distant dreams. Illinois averages 38 inches of annual precipitation. However, during the fourteen years 1886 through 1899, South Dakota averaged only 18.11 inches, less than half of what my ancestors were used to in Illinois.

The last two members of my family's pioneer generation died in 1947 and 1950, so I only have heard second or third hand the accounts of the extended hardships and deprivations during the late 1800s. I will not try to repeat them, since they could have grown or a cynic might claim I was just making them up.

But I will relate the account written by Laura Ingalls Wilder, which has been accepted as factual. Wilder is best known for her series of eight Little House children's books, which were made into a much-loved TV series, *Little House on the Prairie*. The Little House setting is real. While the TV show has the family living in Minnesota, the family moved often during Ingalls Wilder's childhood. Four books are set in De Smet, Kingsbury County, South Dakota, where the Ingall's and later the Wilder's settled. The Little House is just west of DeSmet in Kingsbury County, South Dakota. I have been to the house and walked the fields of the Wilder's former farm. The whole area is now verdant. The land would bring thousands of dollars an acre today. But in 1894, because of drought, it had become worthless.

Laura Ingalls Wilder also wrote non-fiction articles and books. A published diary, entitled *On the Way Home*, told of the loss of the family farm because of an extended drought beginning in 1886. Wilder's account begins,

> For seven years there had been too little rain. The prairies were dust. Day after day, summer after summer, the scorching winds blew the dust and the sun was brassy in a yellow sky. Crop after crop failed. Again and again the barren land must be mortgaged, for taxes and food and next year's seed. The agony of hope ended when there was no harvest and no more credit, no money to pay interest and taxes; the banker took the land. Then the bank failed (p. 1).

On July 17, 1894, the Wilder family loaded their meager belongings into a wagon and began what was called "a trip of desperation" the 650-mile journey to Mansfield, Missouri. There, the Wilders survived and eventually prospered. I have visited the Wilder family graves, homesite, and museum in Mansfield, Missouri.

Writing separately, Wilder's daughter Rose Wilder Lane, also a very successful author in her own right, recounted a folk song entitled "Dakota Land" (n.d.) had sprung from an unknown source. She wrote it was sung widely to the tune of the Christmas carol "Oh Tannenbaum" . . .

> We've reached the land of drought and heat,
> Where nothing grows for man to eat.
> We do not live, we only stay,
> cause we're too poor to get away.

> Dakota Land, sweet Dakota Land,
> As on its burning soil I stand,
> I look across the endless plains,
> And wonder why it never rains.

> We have no corn, we have no oats,
> We have no grain to feed our goats.
> Our pigs go crying down the lane,
> And wonder why it never rains.

> Our horses are the finest race,
> Starvation stares them in the face.
> But with a smile upon our lips,
> We gather up the buffalo chips.

> So on Dakota Land we're going to stay,
> Cause we're too poor to get away.

There is an additional stanza praying for the Angel Gabriel to blow his horn and announce the return of adequate rain.

In should be known that the great drought of the late 1800s in the United States did not spare Canada. From the data available, it seems the drought was even worse in Canada's three prairie provinces than in the United States.

In Winnipeg, Manitoba, precipitation from 1886 through 1895 averaged 18.96 inches, compared to Winnipeg's normal annual total of 20.20 inches. This decade was therefore a period of moderate drought in Winnipeg and it corresponds closely to the shortfall described above in North Dakota during the same years.

Further west in Canada, there was extreme drought, beginning a year earlier in Calgary, Alberta, with only 13.67 inches recorded in 1885. For eleven years, 1885 through 1895, precipitation in Calgary averaged only 12.68 inches. In 1892, Calgary received just 7.91 inches; its next lowest year was 1918, with 9.12 inches. Calgary's normal annual precipitation is 16.68 inches.

Edmonton, Alberta was even drier. The drought there began in 1883, when precipitation totaled only 9.27 inches and continued for sixteen years, through 1898. During that period, precipitation averaged 14.77 inches. It included the two driest years on record, 1889 with 8.16 inches and 1886 with 9.22 inches. Extreme drought lasted through 1898 when 10.90 inches was received, the fifth lowest yearly total in Edmonton's records. Edmonton's normal annual precipitation is 17.69 inches.

Qu'Appelle, Saskatchewan's precipitation records are available beginning in June 1883. Precipitation in the seven months from June through December 1883 was 2.50 inches less than normal, but the annual total is unknown. It is certain, however, that the extreme drought in Qu'Appelle began in 1884 and lasted for twelve years, through 1895. During this period, precipitation averaged 15.13 inches, including the two driest years on record, 1886 with 10.16 inches and 1889 with 10.54 inches. Qu'Appelle's normal precipitation is 18.33 inches per year.

That the great drought began a year or two prior to 1886 in Canada means that if statewide data were available for Idaho and Montana, it would probably show that the drought also arrived there before 1886. As evidence of this, precipitation for individual sites in Montana was as follows during 1885:

- Crow Agency, Big Horn County—9.34 inches

- Miles City, Custer County—10.28 inches

- Helena, Lewis and Clark County—10.99 inches

- Havre, Hill County—8.37 inches

Montana's normal precipitation total is 18.68 inches per year, but all available data for 1885 would point to a statewide total of only about ten inches.

Evidence shows that for much of the western United States and central Canada the drought which began sometime between 1883 to 1886, and continued in some states until as late as 1904, was much more extreme than any seen in the United States and Canada since 1900. What was precipitation in the earlier years of the 19th century? There is enough data available to convince any reasonable person that prior to the period discussed above, precipitation was even less.

As previously mentioned, statewide monthly and annual precipitation records exist for a few states prior to 1886. Missouri has the longest precipitation history. Monthly and annual precipitation amounts have been published by the government, beginning with January 1867. As of 2025, complete precipitation records for Missouri are available for 158 years, much longer than any other state. The driest ten years in Missouri were the decade 1870 to 1879, when precipitation averaged 36.28 inches. The driest twenty-year period in Missouri was from 1870 through 1889, which recorded an average of 37.27 inches per year. And Missouri's driest thirty-year period is the first thirty years available, 1867 through 1896, which averaged 37.86 inches.

Because of the changing climate, Missouri now receives much greater precipitation—during the most recent thirty years, its precipitation averaged 43.58 inches. The record shows that the trend in Missouri toward a drier climate extends back as far as records exist. While this is only one state, there is a positive correlation between precipitation in Missouri and its neighboring states. Similar (but admittedly not identical) dry or wet periods in Iowa, Nebraska, Kansas, and other bordering states always accompany any extended dry (or wet) period in Missouri. There is also a positive relationship between Missouri's precipitation and the entire 48 contiguous states. For example, since 1895, the driest consecutive five-year period for both Missouri and the other 47 states was identical, 1952 through 1956.

The University of Nebraska did an authoritative analysis of the state's precipitation history. In 1935, the university published a study of Nebraska's annual precipitation since the Kansas-Nebraska Act passed in 1854. The study was updated and republished in 1974, with data from 1850 through 1970 in the well-known book *The Climate of the Great American Desert* by Everett Dick. The study found that in Nebraska, by far the driest period from 1850 through 1970 (121 years), was the six consecutive years of drought of 1859 through 1864. Dick wrote extensively about this period in his book. He wrote,

> . . . suddenly a severe drouth pounced down upon them (the settlers) . . . From June 19, 1859, until November 1860 not one good rain fell, and there were but two slight snows in winter. During the summer of 1860, hot winds from the southwest swept the prairies as if the very breath of hell itself had been released.

Dick entitled this chapter "The Great Exodus," because of people leaving the plains saying, "in fact it may be stated without exception that the high plains went broke altogether . . ." Dick continued "Every cloud appearing on the horizon raised hoped for desperate farmers as surely as sight of a sail ever did for shipwrecked sailors on a lonely island."

Finally, in 1952, the U.S. Weather Bureau published a remarkable little book (126 pages) entitled *Climate and Weather in North Dakota*. The section on PRECIPITATION begins with the statement, "Precipitation, which includes rain, snow, hail, sleet, etc., is the most important of all the elements that make up the climate of any locality" (p. 52). This simple truth is lost today in the obsession with temperature. The book produced a table of precipitation by decade, beginning in 1871. North Dakota's average for the ten years 1871–1880 was 16.83 inches, for the decade 1881–1890 the average was 16.63 inches. This provides proof that dry conditions in North Dakota existed prior to the year 1886, as already discussed. Precipitation data for North Dakota prior to 1871 is very limited. Devils Lake in Ramsey County received 15.20 inches in 1870. Buford in Williams County totaled 11.50 inches in 1868, 9.41 inches in 1869, and 9.90 inches in 1870. Garrison in McLean County received 11.13 inches in 1868, 1869 is missing, and 20.27 inches in 1870. This meager data prior to 1871 makes five totals where precipitation was at drought levels and one was above normal.

To document extreme drought beyond the above examples of Missouri, Nebraska, and North Dakota, it is necessary to consult the precipitation records of individual sites. Congress enacted a very important law in February 1870, which provided for the establishment of the first network of official weather stations reporting by telegraph. Believe it or not, the entire act is only one sentence long. For the first several years after passage, the only weather stations in the American West operating under this new law were in Cheyenne, Wyoming and Omaha, Nebraska.

Complete climate records are available for Cheyenne beginning in 1870. Cheyenne's climate is very dry. Over the past 155 years, its precipitation averaged only 14.71 inches. The record clearly proves that Cheyenne experienced extreme drought in the 1800s. Cheyenne's driest year was 1876, with only 5.04 inches. For the first thirteen years of records, 1870 through 1882, Cheyenne's greatest annual precipitation was in 1872 with 13.79 inches. Cheyenne's driest ten years were 1873 through 1882, which averaged only 9.81 inches. Its driest twenty years are the first twenty available, 1870 through 1889, which averaged 11.72 inches and its driest thirty years are also the first thirty on record, 1870 through 1899, which averaged 12.78 inches. Since 1899, there has been a trend toward increased precipitation in Cheyenne. During the most recent thirty years, 1994 through 2023, Cheyenne's precipitation averaged 15.09 inches. In the year 2023, Cheyenne's precipitation totaled 20.37 inches, seventh highest in the 155 years on record.

Saint Paul, Ramsey County, Minnesota precipitation records begin in July 1836. The lowest annual amount received in Saint Paul was a minuscule 10.21 inches in 1910. A year later, in 1911, the total was an amazing 40.49 inches. The 1800s were exceptionally dry in Saint Paul. The second lowest year in its history was 1852, with 15.07 inches. Saint Paul's driest five-year period was 1852 through 1856, which averaged 21.91 inches. 1863 and 1864 were the third and fourth driest years in the city, averaging 15.65 inches. This made them the two driest consecutive years in the past 186 by a very large margin. The next two driest years were 1852 and 1853, which averaged 17.77 inches. Precipitation in Saint Paul has increased tremendously because of the changing climate, particularly during the past forty years. Saint Paul's precipitation now averages over 31 inches per year.

Complete precipitation records by month and year exist for Leavenworth, Kansas, from 1836 through 2024 (189 years). As such, it is the longest record for any site west of the Missouri River. Leavenworth experienced incredible drought in four years:

- 1864—14.60 inches

- 1843—15.94 inches

- 1860—19.19 inches

- 1963—19.78 inches

The driest two consecutive years in Leavenworth were 1846 and 1847, with 21.03 and 23.75 inches. The next driest two consecutive years were 1853 and 1854, with 24.40 and 25.20 inches. The year 1886 was seventh driest with 22.25 inches. Leavenworth's driest five-year period was, as expected, 1860 through 1864, which averaged 24.26 inches. Its driest ten years were 1838 through 1847, which averaged 28.77 inches. Over the entire period of record, Leavenworth has averaged 36.50 inches per year. Any annual total of less than 30 inches is very dry. Across the river, to the east, precipitation records for Miami in Holt County, Missouri, begin in 1847. Its driest year was 1860 with 15.73 inches. As in Leavenworth, its driest two consecutive years were 1853 and 1854, with 21.18 and 23.08 inches. Miami, Missouri's precipitation average is 37.99 inches per year. Manhattan, in Riley County Kansas, records begin in 1858. Manhattan's driest year was 1860 with 15.13 inches, 1864 was 8th driest with 20.25 inches. Several sites with the longest precipitation records in the Great Plains record either 1860 or 1864 as their driest year, each by substantial amounts.

Weather stations in Texas prior to 1886 are rare, but precipitation records for El Paso begin in 1867. Records are missing for four years, but monthly and annual precipitation data is available for 152 complete years. El Paso is extremely dry, averaging only 8.62 inches per year. El Paso's four driest years on record are:

- 1891—2.22 inches
- 1934—2.73 inches
- 1867—2.84 inches
- 1910—4.03 inches

The year 1894 was El Paso's sixth driest with 4.24 inches. Recording sites in New Mexico are also rare, but there are over 150 years of records are available for Albuquerque. Its annual average is 8.63 inches. Most years prior to 1889 are missing, but the average in Albuquerque for the period 1889 through 1904 is only 7.14 inches. Albuquerque's precipitation data confirms the already mentioned megadrought in Arizona, which lasted through 1904.

Turning to drought in the East, which is defined herein as any state east of Illinois, major drought is very rare, less severe, and of short duration. Droughts in the East do not last for decades or even for five years. The 48 states are divided into 344 climate divisions, with states having from one (Rhode Island) to ten divisions. In the East, during the 130 years 1895 through 2024, there are only five instances where precipitation in any climate division was less than twenty inches. The year 1930 has four:

- Michigan Division 7—19.44 inches

- Virginia Division 4—19.47 inches

- Virginia Division 5—19.75 inches

- West Virginia Division 6—18.81 inches

The last example is Michigan Division 10, which had 19.57 inches in 1963. In the four cases seen in 1930, the record drought extended into January and February 1931, with low recorded totals. After these 14-month droughts, precipitation returned to near normal amounts. Maryland Climate Division 4 received only 20.76 inches in 1930, less than half its normal 42.81 inches. Droughts in the East are given below, understanding that any amounts less than or even near to twenty inches are extremely dry.

Burlington, Vermont has precipitation records for 182 years. The driest year in Burlington was 1881 with 20.99 inches, during a highly unusual four-year drought. The year 1879 was 7th driest with 24.27 inches, 1880 was 8th driest with 25.21 inches and 1882 was 10th driest with 25.64 inches. Burlington normally receives 33.75 inches per year.

Charleston, South Carolina has continuous precipitation records beginning in 1832. Normal annual precipitation in Charleston is 48.8 inches. The least annual precipitation in Charleston, by a remarkable amount, was 23.69 inches in 1850. 1849 through 1851 would be by far the driest in Charleston's history. 1849 was the 5th driest year with 30.69 inches and 1851 was the 14th driest, totaling 33.14 inches. The second lowest year was 28.80 inches in 1931.

Rochester in Monroe County, New York, saw two remarkably dry years in its records since 1829. In 1834 there was only 17.04 inches recorded, which may be the single lowest annual total of any published site in the East. The second driest year in Rochester was 1887, which received 20.30 inches. The lowest amount since 1900 was in 1964, with 22.45 inches. Troy in Rensselaer County, New York received 18.32 inches in 1839. Very few sites in the East have ever received less than 20 inches in a year, but the few examples available were all recorded in the 1800s.

Carrollton, the county seat of Carroll County in northern Kentucky, got only 17.49 inches in 1901, less than half its normal 43 inches. This seems to be the lowest annual total ever recorded by an official site in Kentucky, Tennessee, or Ohio. About forty miles northeast of Carrollton, across the Ohio River, Cincinnati in Hamilton County, Ohio, received only 17.99 inches in 1901. Cincinnati's second driest year was 1934 with 22.76 inches. North of Cincinnati, Jacksonburg in Butler County received 22.65 inches in 1901, substantially its driest year. For both Carrollton and Cincinnati, the last four months of 1900, through the first four months of 1902, recorded well below normal precipitation. Thus, it can be fairly said that the record droughts in these two sites covered 20 months. However, the relevant point is major droughts east of Illinois are extremely rare. In studying all published precipitation data available since the early 1800s, there does not appear to be a single site or instance east of Illinois where major drought lasted for over 20 consecutive months.

Washington, DC received only 18.79 inches in 1826, an amount that defies comparison with today's climate. Washington's lowest amount in any year since the 1800s was 21.66 inches in 1930. As mentioned earlier, 1930 was by far the driest year in many eastern states since 1895.

Perhaps the most accepted long-term precipitation record is for Baltimore, Maryland. Records for Baltimore begin in January 1817 and have continued to present, 208 years. The driest year in Baltimore's history was 1930, with 21.55 inches. However, the next six lowest were in the period 1825 through 1870. The two driest consecutive years were 1869 and 1870, which averaged 25.14 inches. The driest five-year period in Baltimore was 1866 through 1870, averaging 28.67 inches. Any year in Baltimore which receives less than 30 inches is considered extremely dry. During the past 208 years, this shortfall has been recorded only 14 times. Tellingly, of Baltimore's 14 extremely dry years, eleven of them occurred in the 1800s. The last unusually dry year in Baltimore was 1991, over thirty years ago, which was 30.16 inches. Like most other sites in North

America, precipitation in Baltimore has increased markedly since 1900. Baltimore now averages approximately 47 inches of precipitation per year.

Two other cities to note are Augusta, Georgia in Richmond County and Philadelphia, Pennsylvania. Augusta received only 19.13 inches in 1845. This appears to be the lowest recorded annual total ever received at a site in the Deep South in the United States. Philadelphia received 23.25 inches in 1819. Since 1900, the least precipitation received was 29.31 inches in 1922.

The preceding paragraphs summarize drought in the eastern United States. There have also been periods which were considered abnormally dry, such as the years 1960 through 1966 in New York State. In 1964, New York State received only 31.56 inches of precipitation. This shortfall was merely an inconvenience, not a true drought.

There is a reason climate activists rarely mention drought or deem it to be a very important factor. Mostly, these people live in the eastern United States and the simple truth is neither they nor their ancestors have ever lived through a drought worthy of the name. The East has never had a real drought. In the Great Plains, the most important climate factor, by far, is precipitation. Folks in the center of the nation rejoice that climate change has resulted in increased precipitation—from a low of only 10.90 inches in South Dakota in 1936, increasing almost steadily to a wonderful 31.39 inches in 2019. Naturally, Dakotans are content to let the climate activists complain about small increases in temperature.

Climate and drought dominate the setting in John's Steinbeck's 1939 novel *The Grapes of Wrath*. But another of his works, *East of Eden*, published in 1952, contains an excellent excerpt on the subject. Writing of the Salinas Valley (Monterey County) California (158,693 square miles), where Steinbeck grew up in the early 1900s, he related,

> I have spoken of the rich years when the rain was plentiful. But there were dry years too, and they put a terror on the valley. The water came in a thirty-year cycle. There would be five of six wet

and wonderful years when there might be nineteen to twenty-five inches of rain, and the land would shout with grass. Then would come six or seven pretty good years of twelve to sixteen inches of rain. And then the dry years would come, and sometimes there would be only seven or eight inches of rain. The land dried up and the grasses headed out miserably a few inches high and great bare scabby places appeared in the valley. The live oaks got a crusty look and the sagebrush was gray. The land cracked and the springs dried up and the cattle listlessly nibbled dry twigs. Then the farmers and the ranchers would be filled with disgust for the Salinas Valley. The cows would grow thin and sometimes starve to death. People would have to haul water in barrels to their farms just for drinking. Some families would sell out for nearly nothing and move away. And it never failed that during the dry years the people forgot about the rich years, and during the wet years they lost all memory of the dry years. It was always that way (p. 5).

I must interject here to state that drought is never universal—extreme drought may cover more than a million square miles, but there is always a boundary. Beyond this line, normal or above normal precipitation is received. This was seen in California during the late 1800s. The Great Drought I have documented did not extend to California. Complete precipitation records are available for Sacramento, San Francisco, and San Diego beginning in 1850. Excellent records for Red Bluff (Tehama County) and Fresno begin in 1878 and there are other sites. From 1850 through 1899, over a fifty-year period, California saw only the drought normally expected. In the ten years I have mentioned frequently for other states, 1886 through 1895, precipitation in six of the years was above normal and below normal in four. In fact, the year 1889 was one of the ten or twelve wettest years in California's history.

Let us return to what John Steinbeck observed. This is exactly what is happening today, as no one remembers or even acknowledges the great droughts and drier climate of the 1800s. It seems this is intentional. It serves the interests of the climate cultists to ignore (or even deny) the extreme and unprecedented droughts that plagued much of the nation in the 19th century. If they admit that precipitation has increased since 1900, the carefully constructed narrative they wish to present will be threatened. Climate change cannot successfully be portrayed as an unmitigated horror if untidy facts like the wonderful increase in precipitation since 1900 may become part of the story.

The presentation of climate change as an unalloyed crisis is just fine with the media. Simple stories are easier to deliver and promote and the press is thrilled to go along with the climate cultists claim that the climate was benign in the past but is now going to hell. No one in the media fact checks anything, nor do any of them even know how. Today's journalists have readily accepted the instruction William Randolph Hearst gave to his reporters, "Always remember men, too much checking of the facts will ruin a good story." So the incessant scare-mongering by the press continues, growing more strident and hysterical with each passing year.

But if the truth about drought in the 1800s were included, the true picture would be much more complicated to present. It would be unpleasant to recall and report that drought and dry conditions in the 1800s resulted in suffering, bankruptcies, depopulation, and hardships much greater than any seen since. To the contrary, the present climate trends are supposedly going to lead to these results. Never mind the *inconvenient truth* that the major increases in precipitation over the past 130 years have resulted in great wealth and prosperity in most of the United States and Canada.

As I have shown, extreme drought plagued much of North America in the 1800s. But it was accompanied and enhanced by the second major feature of the climate—intense cold. Part 2 of this study will concern temperature and document how incredibly cold it was in the 1800s. Considering both the extreme drought and intense cold of the 19th century, we can be delighted we are now spared the climatic conditions North America endured in the 1800s.

PART II

Temperature

NOTE: All temperatures are in degrees Fahrenheit unless otherwise noted.

As we go back prior to 1900 in North America, and in fact the entire world, temperatures were much colder than today. This is not a controversial statement. Anyone who has studied climate history for even a brief time knows that the 1800s and earlier were part of the period known as the Little Ice Age. The world was much colder during this era, which extended (with much debate as to its exact beginning and end) from around the year 1300 to at least 1850. Two excellent books on this important period are by Dr. Brian M. Fagan, professor emeritus of the University of California, entitled *The Little Ice Age: How Climate Made History 1300–1850,* and *The Long Summer: How Climate Changed Civilization.* For a thorough understanding of the Little Ice Age, read both.

To provide a frame of reference for examining the data on temperature in the 1800s, a few basic facts about more recent temperatures are provided. The average temperature in the 48 contiguous states over the past 130 years, 1895 through 2024, has been 52.29°. The warmest year was 2024, which averaged 55.50°, and the coolest was 1917 with 50.05°. The details and consequences of 2024 will be discussed below. Oddly, the warmest month ever recorded in the CONUS was July 1936 with 76.77°.

The coldest month was January 1979, which averaged only 21.92°. February 1936 in North Dakota was the coldest month in any state, which averaged a very polar minus 14.1°. The hottest month seen in any state was Oklahoma in July 2011, when the temperature averaged a sweltering 89.2°. During the past 130 years, the CONUS has warmed at a rate of 1.72 degrees per century.

As stated above, the year 2024, which averaged 55.50°, was the warmest year in the past 130. As such, it deserves to be examined in some detail. For context, the second warmest year in the CONUS was 2012, which averaged 55.27°, and the third warmest was 2016, which averaged 54.90°. These three years were considerably warmer than any of the remaining 127 years. None of the 12 months during 2024 were the warmest on record, but the temperature in every month was considerably above average. It was not remarkably hot during either July or August. The greatest heat waves of a month or longer since 1895 were in July and August 2011, or in several states as early as July 1936. The unusually warm months in 2024 were:

- February—third warmest
- June—second warmest
- September—second warmest
- October—second warmest
- December—fourth warmest

These five months of near record warmth, when combined with the seven remaining months which were all above normal, resulted in 2024 being the warmest year yet seen in the 48 states.

Digging deeper into the month-by-month data for 2024 reveals some very interesting and thought- provoking details. For each month, the year and temperature will be provided for the three (or more) warmest years on record. I will begin with June, the first summer month. The national average temperature in June 2024 was 71.80°. The warmest June was 2021 with 72.57°. The third warmest was June 2016, with 71.74°. Certainly, on a national scale, the June 2024 average temperature of 71.80° was not oppressively warm.

But in a few of the states, June 2024 was hot, at least to some extent. In Arizona, June 2024 averaged 80.4°, second only to the 80.6° average of June 2021. New Mexico had its warmest June on record in 2024 with 74.8°. The second warmest June was 1990, which averaged 74.5°.

In California, the June 2024 temperature averaged 74.1°, its third warmest, behind June 2021 with 74.9° and June 2015 with 74.4°. The temperature in Texas in June 1924 was the warmest of any state, with an average of 83.3°. This was the eighth warmest June in Texas, and considerably below the 85.2° of June 2011, the 85.0° in June 1953 and five other years. In Oklahoma, June 2024 was the eleventh warmest on record, with 80.4° and was much below the June averages of:

- 1953—84.7°
- 1911—83.8°
- 2011—83.4°
- Plus seven other years

In Kansas, the June 2024, temperature averaged 77.2°, which was its 14th warmest June since 1895. It has been much hotter in prior Junes:

- 1952—81.2°
- 1953—80.7°
- 1933—80.3°
- 1934—79.9°
- 1911—79.3°

The book *Climate of Kansas,* published by Kansas State University, says that in June 1890, the temperature averaged 77.6°. Finally, to be complete, in Missouri, the June 2024 temperature averaged 75.8°, which was its 18th warmest since 1895. This compares to 80.0° in 1952, 79.7° in both 1934 and June 1953, 78.8° in 1914, 78.5° in 1911, etc., etc. This is the entire list of the states in which June 2024 could, according to any criteria, be considered hot.

The people of New Mexico (and the other states) can say if their record June temperature of 74.8° constituted a problem worth mentioning. Although June 2024 was the second warmest on record for the nation, when examined, it is difficult to find examples of states which suffered because of the near record June warmth.

At the opposite end of the list are a long series of specific examples where the much above average temperatures of June 2024 could be welcome and beneficial. I will provide just three.

1. Idaho: The June 2024 temperature averaged 60.2°, which was 3.2° above its 130-year average of 57.0°.

2. Colorado: The average was 66.7° in June 2024. This was 5.0° above its long-term June average of 61.7°.

3. Maine: The June 2024 temperature averaged 63.9°, which was 3.9° higher than its average of 60.0°.

Climate change activists consistently present the warming climate as an unmitigated horror story; could the truth be that warmer temperatures are preferred by many (perhaps even a majority) of the residents of the cooler states? Perhaps the residents of Idaho, Colorado, and Maine (and at least 20 more states) appreciate not needing to run their furnaces as much, if at all, during June 2024. This is an actual possibility that should be seriously entertained. But the climate crazies and their enablers in the media will not allow any such ideas to be considered. All warming must be portrayed as destructive. Never mind the obvious truth that in June 2024, throughout much of the nation, the near record warmth in the

United States was a welcome event. Having now scrutinized the one relatively warm month of 2024, I will provide summaries of 2024's other notably warm months, February, September, October, and December.

First, February 2024 was the third warmest February in the past 130 years, during which the temperature averaged 40.82° in the CONUS. February 1954 was the warmest on record with 41.41° average, and the second warmest was 2017, which averaged 41.16°. The coldest February since 1895 in the 48 states was February 1936, which averaged 25.23°, followed by February 1899 with an average of 25.50°. During the past 130 years, February temperatures have warmed at a rate of 3.07 degrees per century, a much faster rate of warming than any other month. As with June, the most interesting and informative data is found in the temperature records of several states.

The near record warmth of February 2024 was concentrated near the center of the United States, where February temperatures are usually colder than the national average. In fact, Iowa and Missouri saw their warmest Februarys on record in 2024. It was the second warmest February in the past 130 years in Illinois, Indiana, Michigan, Minnesota, Ohio, and Wisconsin. We will look at Iowa and Minnesota as representative of the group of states, which were unusually warm in February 2024.

February 2024 was remarkably warm in Iowa where the temperature averaged 37.0°, which was an amazing 1.4° warmer than the previous record 35.6° average in 1954. Iowa's coldest February since 1895 was in 1936, during which the temperature averaged a frigid 4.4°. An open-minded person would consider this data and wonder which is best for Iowa—a winter month averaging only 4.4° or 37.0°? The residents of Iowa should be allowed to answer this for themselves, without interference from outsiders. The same goes true for Minnesota and all other states. In Minnesota, the temperature in February 2024 averaged 28.2°, a little below the previous high-temperature average of 28.8° in February 1998. The coldest February in Minnesota since 1895 was in 1936, during which the temperature averaged an absolutely polar minus 7.2°. In Minnesota, February temperatures have increased at a very rapid rate of 4.9 degrees per century over the past 130 years. Not even the most stubborn and obtuse climate activists could put together an argument claiming the warming of February temperatures in Iowa, Minnesota, and other similar states is a harmful trend. Warmer February's are not destructive. They are exactly the opposite—relief from the extreme cold of the past has been a wonderful blessing and will continue to be. There are those who will disagree with this conclusion. That is your right. But those who disagree do not have the right to tell the residents of Iowa or any state what is harmful or what is beneficial for them. Each state, indeed each person, has a fundamental *God-given* right to decide these matters for themselves. In my opinion it logically follows that, if I have the right to decide what climate is best for someone else, then it is a very short and logical step for me to claim that I also have the right to force them to take actions, or refrain from taking actions, as I dictate. Climate cultists are certainly this arrogant. They claim they have the divine right to impose their favored policies on others, even if it can clearly be shown that these policies are contrary to others' preferences, wishes, and best interests.

In September 2024, the average temperature in the 48 states was 68.63°, second only to the 68.95° average of September 1998. The coldest Septembers in the past 130 years in the CONUS were September 1965 with 61.75° and September 1918 with 61.90°. September temperatures have warmed at a rate of 1.36 degrees per century, less than half as fast as in February. The unusual warmth in September was concentrated in the north central part of the United States. Minnesota, North Dakota, South Dakota, and Wyoming experienced their warmest Septembers in 2024. Normally September weather is very pleasant in the Great Plains, but there have been some exceptions—all because of the unexpected cold.

I'll use my home state, South Dakota, as the example for September 2024. The contrasts I provide for South Dakota were even greater in Minnesota, North Dakota, and Wyoming. The temperature in South Dakota averaged 68.2° during September 2024. This was 0.5° warmer than the previous record, 67.7° of September 1897. South Dakota was, by a large margin, the warmest of the four states listed. For comparison, in September 2024, Wyoming averaged only 60.0°. The coldest September in South

Dakota since 1895 was 1965, when the temperature averaged only 49.6°.
I believe my family members still in South Dakota would report that
last September's average temperature of 68.2° was about perfect. Like the
porridge Goldilocks finally ate, it was not too hot and not too cold—it
was just right.

In the northern plains, the problem with below normal temperatures in
the fall is the danger of early freezes which damage crops not yet harvested.
With an average temperature of 49.6° for the month in September 1965,
there is a very high likelihood that hard killing freezes occurred overnight
on more than one occasion. That, and for city folks, the irritation of having to use their home's furnaces a month or so earlier than expected. I do
not know the extent of early freezes and resulting damage in the northern
plains during the record cold September 1965. I was seventeen that year
and I remember it was windy and cold. Pheasant hunts with my new
Winchester Model 59 were lousy—the ringnecks stayed hidden in their
cover and refused to be flushed as hunters walked along the fence lines. As
in February, it is difficult to conclude that the temperature in September
2024 was so warm that it caused damage and economic loss. However,
the opposite is a known fact—a cold September in the upper plains is
both costly and unpleasant. Given the choice of a September averaging
68.2° or 49.6°, a vast majority of the residents of South Dakota would
choose the former. Secretly, most would probably wish for Septembers to
be even a degree or two warmer than 68°.

As in September, October 2024 was the second warmest yet seen in the
contiguous 48 states. The average temperature was 58.96°, second only to
October 1963, which averaged 59.34°. October has warmed quite slowly,
at a rate of only 1.06 degrees per century over the past 130 years. The
coldest October on record was in 1925, which averaged 48.92°. The unusual warmth of October 2024 was in the southwestern states. Arizona,
New Mexico, Texas, and Utah all had record warmth in October 2024.
Colorado's average in September was 52.7°, one tenth of a degree less than
the 52.8° average of October 1963. Wyoming's average in October 2024
was 48.9°, three-tenths of a degree less than the 49.2° average in October
1963. Which temperature is best for Utah, for example? October 2024,

which averaged 55.9° or its coldest October 1919, which averaged only 41.8°? Would Texans prefer the 72.9° average of October 2024 or the 58.3° average recorded in October 1976? And which might the residents of Wyoming like best, the 48.9° seen in October 2024 or the near freezing 33.2° average of 1919? But of course I am being a little facetious. No one in their right mind would say that an average October temperature less than 40.0° in Wyoming would be preferable to an average above 45.0°. To the climate change activists, warmer temperatures are always a problem. They channel the Marxist philosopher Jean Paul Sartre and frequently claim that all warming is *an existential threat to civilization*. Whatever that ridiculous word salad precisely means cannot be determined. People who pay heating bills, harvest crops, care for livestock, and otherwise live in the real world have a right to disagree. They do not need to be told what is good for them by those who have never walked a mile in their shoes.

December 2024 was the fourth warmest in the CONUS in the past 130 years. All four of the unusually warm Decembers have been in the most recent ten years. December 2024 temperature averaged 38.17°. December temperatures have warmed nicely over the period of record at a rate of 2.51 degrees per century. The coldest December since 1895 was in 1983, which averaged 25.48°. I lived in Nebraska during 1983 and December of that year can only be described as horribly cold, averaging only 7.9°. In South Dakota, December 1983 averaged 2.0°, and in North Dakota, the average was minus 2.6°. Minnesota temperatures averaged minus 0.8°. Montana, the average was 3.4°, Iowa averaged 7.6°, and Wisconsin averaged 6.9°. As expected, December 1983 was even colder in Canada. For example, the average in Winnipeg, Manitoba, was minus 4.4° and Calgary, Alberta averaged minus 3.3°. Across more than a million square miles in the middle of North America, the record cold of December 1983 was costly, destructive, and miserable. I will not waste time and ink documenting how terrible such an extreme December cold can be, or how beneficial the much warmer December temperatures have been in recent years.

Besides a month-by-month analysis, the states with record high temperatures in 2024 should be considered. Maine is a good example. In 2024,

Maine temperatures averaged 44.98°, which was 0.35° warmer than the previous record of 44.63° in 2010. The only near record warm month in Maine in 2024 was November, which averaged 38.7°. The warmest November in Maine was 2006, which averaged 38.9°. By any reasonable criteria, the temperature in Maine in 2024 was still cold. And only the citizens of Maine may say if they prefer the 44.98° average of 2024 or if they would like to return to the 36.52° average of 1904. The same comparisons can be made for Michigan, Minnesota, Wisconsin, and others.

This analysis of the record high temperature of 2024 in the United States shows that while it is easy to consider this to be bad news, an examination of the unusual warmth will lead thinking persons to reconsider this conclusion. In June, the only state where the temperature can honestly be classified as hot was Arizona. In the four other months which were near record high temperatures, February, September, October, and December, only the most contrived interpretation of the data might say this was adverse or damaging. The reasonable interpretation of these four months is that their unusual warmth was, on balance, pleasant and very beneficial. Of course, this could be debated, but it should be remembered that only the residents of the states or provinces in Canada can say what temperatures are preferable and good for them. Any would be self-appointed experts from elsewhere have no say in the matter.

To return to the subject of historical temperatures, extremes were recorded in the nation's 344 climate divisions. This says volumes about the amazing variety and range of temperatures in North America. Temperatures matter for the individual climate divisions because that might be where *you* live. For my purposes, I define hot as whenever the temperature for a month averages higher than 80.0° and extremely hot is a monthly average higher than 90.0°. Cold is an average below 32.0° for a month and extremely cold as average temperatures below zero degrees for a month. Others may define hot and cold differently, but my suggested boundaries allow objective analysis and provide some perspective. Hot temperatures are easier to summarize. States like North and South Dakota have both seen only one hot month, July 1936, since their records began in the late 1800s. More importantly, NO state has ever seen an extremely hot month.

However, there are quite a few examples when a climate division averaged extremely hot temperatures. Most occurred within the past five or six years. Here are a few outstanding examples.

- **Arizona Climate Divisions 4 and 5**

The highest average monthly temperature ever recorded was in Arizona Climate Division 5 (10,015 square miles, Southwest) in July 2024 when the temperature averaged 97.3°. The temperature in Climate Division 5 in July 2023 averaged 97.0°. Arizona Climate Division 4 (14,649 square miles, South Central) averaged 95.1° in July 2023 and 94.0° in July 2024. Extreme heat is the norm for July and August in these parts of Arizona, which are famous (or notorious) for their high temperatures. The mean temperature for July in the 130 years, 1895–2024, in Arizona's Climate Division 5 is 91.4° and the mean for the period in August is 90.2°. Yet people freely choose to live in these extreme and potentially lethal environments. I am reminded of the line from Noël Coward's comic song "Mad Dogs and Englishmen go out in the midday sun." Coward's daft colonial rulers of Burma and the Malay States do not compare to the loonies who inhabit the hellishly hot parts of Arizona.

- **California's Climate Division 7**

California's Climate Division 7 (45,640 square miles, Southeast) is also known as the Southeast Desert Basin. It averaged 91.6° in July 2024.

- **Nevada, Climate Division 4**

In Nevada, Climate Division 4 (9,794 square miles, Extreme Southern) has recorded three cases of an extremely hot month. In Division 4, the temperature averaged 92.7° in July 2024, 91.3° in July 2023 and 90.6° in July 1931.

- **Oklahoma Climate Divisions 7 and 8**

Oklahoma Climate Division 7 (6,922 square miles, Southwest) averaged 91.7° during July 2011 and it continued to be extremely hot in August when the temperature averaged 91.4°. Oklahoma Climate Division 8 (8,425 Square Miles, South Central) averaged 90.5° and 90.8° in July and August 2011.

- **Texas Climate Division 3**

The extremely hot August 2011 temperature extended south into Texas gigantic Climate Division 3 (39,005 Square Miles, North Central) which averaged 91.1° during that month.

I interject briefly here with a small sample of the extreme temperatures recorded in Alaska. Data for Alaska is now available for one hundred years, 1925 through 2024. The coldest months in Alaska were . . .

- January 2012—minus 12.8°
- January 1934—minus 12.1°
- January 1989—minus 11.9 °
- January 1971—minus 11.8°

The warmest months in Alaska in the past hundred years were . . .

- July 2011—58.1°
- July 2004—57.3°
- July 1993—56.8°

Examples of cold temperatures in the CONUS are so common they cannot be listed. Even the category extreme cold has fifty-nine cases when an entire state averaged below zero degrees temperature during a month. There are even instances when a state averaged below zero degrees for two consecutive months. There are 674 cases when a climate division experienced extreme below zero degrees cold for a month since 1895. All but a dozen are in the distant past. For example, North Dakota Climate Division 2 (7088 Square Miles, North Central) averaged minus 11.3° in January 1936, followed by an even more frigid minus 16.9° in February. Sometimes the average temperature in a state is a little misleading. In January 1912, the temperature in Michigan averaged 4.0°, which was pretty darn cold. But during that month, Michigan's Climate Division 1 (9943 Square Miles, West Upper) experienced extreme cold since its temperature averaged minus 6.2°

Canada, as far as I can determine, has never recorded a single case where the temperature qualifies as hot. Records for each site in Canada must be searched since national records do not extend as far back into the 1800s as in the United States. Toronto records begin in 1840. The warmest month in Toronto was July 1921, when the temperature averaged 77.8°. July 1921 also appears to be the warmest month in Montreal, averaging 76.2° with records beginning in 1873. Winnipeg records begin in 1872. Its warmest month was July 1936, which averaged 75.5°. This corresponds to the July 1936 hot month in North Dakota. Canada's examples of temperature averaging below zero degrees in a month are too many to cite.

I will elaborate below, but in summary, the climate of North America is very cold. I will prove that it was much colder in the 1800s than it is now. Why we do not consider relief from the extreme cold of the past to be a benefit strikes me as very odd, to say the least.

Using my definition, Mississippi has only recorded one cold month in the 137 years of records from 1888 through 2024. The coldest month was January 1940, when the temperature averaged 31.7°. Alabama, to the east, has never recorded a cold month. Its lowest temperature average is 32.1°, also in January 1940. Obviously, as with precipitation, the terms cold or hot are location dependent. For example, in North Dakota, the *warmest* January on record from 1892 through 2024 was January 2006, which averaged 25.9°.

The intense cold of the 1800s had three unique aspects. First, it was cold for far longer. Cold temperatures arrived much earlier in the fall and departed later in the spring. Second, temperatures during the very long winters were much lower than those recorded since 1900. Third, intense and long-lasting cold occurred much further to the south.

To illustrate the first of these factors, we need only to return to 1899 and examine the last month of winter for that year. March 1899 was the coldest in 127 years by wide margins in Minnesota, North Dakota, South Dakota, Wisconsin, the Upper Peninsula of Michigan, eastern Montana, northwestern Iowa, and central Canada. The following data gives the average temperature in the four states mentioned in the table below, along with the second and third coldest and finally their warmest March. All four states saw March 2012 as their warmest March on record, as did much of the rest of North America. It is testimony to the courage and endurance of the people in these four states that they could survive and then recover from the tremendously warm temperatures of March 2012. Tragically, in 2012, even North Dakota averaged above 40.0°. We have become spoiled and are now used to March being the first month of spring. This is because the last extremely cold March in the contiguous 48 states was March 1965, 60 years ago.

YEAR	Minnesota	YEAR	N. Dakota	YEAR	S. Dakota	YEAR	Wisconsin
1899	10.90	1899	7.00	1899	14.70	1899	17.40
1965	14.50	1951	11.70	1965	19.20	1960	18.50
1923	15.50	1965	13.70	1951	19.50	1906	20.00
2012	41.80	2012	40.60	2012	47.00	2012	45.60
Std DEV	-2.68	Std DEV	-2.89	Std DEV	-2.90	Std DEV	-2.25

Right away, this data gives an initial hint that temperatures in the 1800s could be (and indeed were) a great deal colder than any recorded in the 20th and 21st centuries. Plus, this is only looking at one month and year. A gap between the coldest year and the second coldest of more than one degree is almost unheard of, much less a difference of over four degrees seen in two of the states above. Standard deviation analysis was done in all four states. The March 1899 temperatures were over two standard deviations below the mean of the 126-year period, 1899 through 2024. Without reservation, this is extraordinary.

Digging into the details a little further, *from a relative standpoint*, the coldest of the cold temperatures in March 1899 were in northern parts of the above areas. For example, North Dakota is divided into nine climate divisions, three northern, three central and three southern. As expected, the average temperatures in the three northern divisions were lower than in the three southern. In addition, in the north, there was a *greater difference* between 1899 and the next coldest years. The average temperature in the North Central climate division was 3.4° in 1899 and the second coldest was 1951, which averaged 9.1°, or 5.7° warmer. The South Central climate division averaged 7.4° in March 1899, while March 1951, the second coldest, averaged 12.9°, or 4.5° warmer. So the northern divisions were both absolutely and proportionally the coldest. This analysis is accurate for all four of the states documented above.

As expected, the most extreme cold in March 1899 was found further north in Canada. Winnipeg, Manitoba, averaged 3.2° in March 1899. Its second coldest was March 1923 with 6.5°. Qu'Appelle, Saskatchewan, averaged only 1.3° in March 1899. Since then, its next coldest was 8.3° in March 1904. Edmonton, Alberta, averaged 8.5° in March 1899, its second coldest was 11.5° in March 1904. Calgary, Alberta, averaged 8.8° in March 1899. Its next coldest was 13.3° in March 1904. Throughout Manitoba, Saskatchewan, and Alberta, March 1899 was colder than any March since then by an average of over three degrees.

March 1899 was much colder than anyone alive today has experienced in an area larger than 500,000 square miles of North America. We will soon return to March and see it was even colder earlier in the 1800s than in 1899.

The second chart shows how winter often arrived early in the 1800s and then hung around like an uninvited guest for the next several months. November 1896 was the coldest on record in Iowa, Minnesota, North Dakota, South Dakota, eastern Montana, much of Nebraska and Wyoming, and central Canada. The following table shows the temperature in four states in November 1896, their next two coldest years since then, and each state's warmest November in the period 1896 through 2024.

YEAR	Iowa	YEAR	Minnesota	YEAR	N. Dakota	YEAR	S. Dakota
1896	27.30	1896	14.80	1896	6.10	1896	14.40
1959	27.60	1911	17.90	1985	13.40	1985	17.50
1911	28.20	1985	18.80	1955	14.30	1955	21.70
2001	48.00	2001	40.70	2016	39.30	1999	42.40

From personal experience, I can vouch that an early onset of winter is almost universally despised and even feared, except perhaps by those in the business of selling space heaters or repairing furnaces. A balmy Indian Summer-type November is very welcome. One might ask the residents of Minnesota if they would prefer next November to be 14.8° as in 1896 or the 40.7° experienced in 2001. Of course, I jest. What ordinary folks might prefer is immaterial to the self-appointed experts. Our betters will decide what climate is good for us whether we like it or not. After all, it is not as if we live in a democracy.

The details of the great cold of November 1896 are quite similar to those in March 1899. The coldest temperatures, in both the relative and absolute sense, were in the northern sections of the four states charted above. North Dakota Climate Division 2 (North Central) recorded an absurd average of 2.4° in November 1896. Division 2's next coldest year was 1985, which averaged 11.7°, or 9.3° warmer. In contrast, North Dakota's South Central Division 8 averaged 6.9° in 1896 but 14.7° in 1985, a difference of 7.8°. One of the standard deviations calculated for the temperature in November 1896 was 3.75 SD below the mean of the 129-year period of 1896 through 2024. This is remarkable, as such extreme standard deviations over a large geographic area should not be seen in a period of less than several hundred years.

The temperature data from individual climate sites is just as startling. For example, monthly temperature records for Havre, Hill County, Montana begin in 1880. Since 1880, the coldest November in Havre was 1896, averaging a frigid 3.8°. The second coldest was 1985, with 9.1°, and the third coldest was 1955 with 13.6°. The warmest November in Havre was in 1949 with 42.9°. If the residents of Havre could pick from the two historical extremes, 3.8 or 42.9°, for next November, which would a majority of them choose?

Since about 1990, we have become used to winters which are three months long. Intense cold is now rare, and such cold spells are only a month long, with very few exceptions. Winters were completely different in the 1800s.

Winter arrived in November and stayed through March. In some notable cases, winter began in mid-October and did not depart until early April.

Monthly and annual temperature data is available for Iowa beginning in January 1873 and for Nebraska beginning in January 1876. While these states are far from the coldest in the contiguous 48, they prove that in the last quarter of the 19th century, winters were longer and colder than those since 1900. The following table gives the coldest five-month winters (November through March) over the past 152 years in Iowa. Last, the table gives the warmest winter ever recorded in Iowa for the five months November through March.

YEAR(S)	NOV	DEC	JAN	FEB	MAR	AVG
1874-75	32.90	24.00	4.90	6.40	26.90	19.02
1880-81	25.30	16.10	9.60	17.00	27.10	19.02
1898-99	30.90	16.80	18.20	11.20	23.40	20.10
1911-12	28.20	26.30	2.40	16.70	23.80	19.48
1978-79	35.00	19.30	4.60	10.70	31.80	20.28
2011-12	39.40	29.10	26.50	29.60	51.60	35.24

Sharp-eyed readers will note that Iowa's November 1880 temperature was only 25.30° while previously the record cold in Iowa, November 1896, was 27.30°. This is correct. November 1880 was 2.0° colder in Iowa than in November 1896. Further west, November 1880 can only be described as crazy cold. As just one example, Denver, Colorado's November 1880 temperature averaged 21.7°. The second coldest November in Denver was 9.3° warmer at 31.0°. November 1880 was the coldest November in the past 152 years in Boise, ID, Nashville, TN, Santa Fe, NM, Marquette, MI, and all points in between. We are on notice that by retreating further into the 1800s; we will find the intensely cold temperatures of the 1890s are eclipsed again and again.

The table below gives the same data for Nebraska, except that, unfortunately, 1874-75 temperatures are not available. I lived in Nebraska for over thirty years from 1973 through 2007 and thus observed the last two winters listed, the freezing winter of 1978-1979 and the record warm winter of 1999-2000. I worked as a fiscal officer for the State Department of Health and Human Services during these years. In the cold winter of 1978-1979, when the temperature averaged 22.66°, we depleted our budgets for heating state institutions and buildings along with the funds in grant programs designated to assist low-income Nebraskans with paying their energy bills. For both shortfalls, we *robbed Peter to pay Paul* by diverting funds from the Repair and Maintenance budgets for buildings and other grant programs to cover the much-needed assistance in paying home heating bills. It was difficult and there was a high price to pay. During the record warm winter of 1999-2000, when the temperature averaged 36.60°, businesses, governments, and families all saw much lower utility bills. Besides saving everyone money, the warmer winter was significantly nicer.

YEAR(S)	NOV	DEC	JAN	FEB	MAR	AVG
1880-81	23.20	16.90	10.80	18.20	30.30	19.88
1898-99	29.80	21.60	21.40	10.40	25.40	21.72
1911-12	30.10	23.20	12.20	25.00	23.00	22.70
1978-79	33.60	18.50	7.80	17.30	36.10	22.66
1999-00	45.00	32.50	28.60	35.00	41.90	36.60

Tables of numbers, such as those above, probably seem sterile and abstract. Mere numbers hide the consequences of intense cold. Therefore, I will briefly depart from mind-numbing data to quote from a personal account of the horrors of the winter of 1880-1881 in Iowa.

The account was written by a pioneer of northwestern Iowa, Thomas Barry of O'Brien County, and published in 1923 in the Iowa Historical Society's quarterly journal, *The Palimpsest* (since renamed *Iowa Heritage Illustrated*). I provide excerpts below. The entire account is in the public domain. Therefore, I recommend anyone willing to have a reality check about the trials and sufferings of a long winter should read the complete article.

Mr. Barry begins his account on the morning of October 15, 1880, when he and his wife struck out by wagon for the town of Sheldon, twelve miles from their farm. The morning was cloudy and calm, but the air was thick with wild ducks and geese flying swiftly southward. Was this an omen for what was to come? They were shopping for their winter supplies when the snow began to fall about two o'clock. By five, when they were ready to begin their return, the wind had risen. Mr. Barry writes,

> The snow that had already fallen was picked up and driven through the air with such terrific force that our horses refused to face the gale. Thinking of the children at home (the oldest being eleven) we urged them on, but they would not budge. Not until then did we fully realize that a blizzard was upon us, and that we would be forced to remain in town until it was over. We could hear the wind moaning around the rude hotel all night, the windows rattled in their loose frames and we could not sleep. "God will care for our children" repeated my wife while my thoughts strayed also to our unprotected stock . . . The blizzard raged fiercely that night and all the next day. But the second morning dawned calm and clear . . . With our rested horses we headed for home, but the low heavy wagon was clumsy in the deep snow. Before we had gone very far the horses floundered and the wagon stuck in a deep drift. For a little while I sat there, overcome . . . we plowed and shoveled our way on. The sun rose high and then began to descend, our fear for those at home became more haunting. Our team became more exhausted with the heavy pulling and lack of food. Finally as the sun was setting over the white prairie, we came in sight of our place. We knew it was our home not by any familiar object but by its position from the road. Nothing was to be seen but the tops of the highest trees. In the middle of the yard was a drift as high as the house. We worked around it in a few minutes and reached the door. Inside we found the children safe but crying bitterly because they were sure we must be dead.

Thus began a winter of hell for Iowa and indeed the entire Great Plains. It lasted until April. Barry went on . . .

> It snowed about twice a week all winter. As the winter wore on, my oats ran out. Only my seed corn remained and it would not go far . . . the pigs squealed with hunger . . . my wife said, "feed them the corn, but do not let them starve" which I did. During that terrible winter we had no wood or coal for fuel . . . My children, usually healthy, took sick in mid-winter. We had no money but I sold our precious eggs and butter for medicine . . . since we had no fuel, I was forced to burn the rest of our seed corn to warm the house. My wife had exhausted her strength caring for the children and became ill . . .

Barry continues for many pages, telling how the family barely survived the next five months. Many others did not survive. "When spring finally arrived, we shook off our comas and emerged like badgers from holes on the prairie. But the unharvested corn in the fields had rotted and become soft. Neither livestock nor poultry would eat it."

Laure Ingalls Wilder wrote an entire book about the winter of 1880-1881 entitled *The Long Winter*. In truth, conditions were even worse in the Dakota Territory. In 1880, the area was sparsely populated. There was little community support and no help or relief from the Territorial Government in Yankton. The main weather station for the Dakota Territory had been established in Yankton in 1873. Yankton is 105 miles south of DeSmet, where the Ingalls's farm was located. I have summarized the lowest temperatures recorded in Yankton over the winter of 1880-1881, below. The low in October 1880 was 15°, which was unusually cold. In some years, Yankton does not record its first freezing temperatures until November. The incredible cold arrived in November 1880, when the low was minus 5.0°. In December, the low reached minus 19°. January 1881's low was minus 32°, February's was minus 23°, March was minus 8.0° and even in April the low was minus 3.0°. Below negative temperatures were recorded in Yankton for six consecutive months from November 1880 through April 1881! Of course, it was even colder in DeSmet and else-where throughout the Dakota Territory than in Yankton, on the south-eastern border.

In 2008, my hometown's newspaper, the Daily Capitol Journal of Pierre, South Dakota, in cooperation with the South Dakota State Historical Society, published a history of Pierre's first 125 years. One major article is entitled "Hard Winter Leads to Year of Destruction for Young City." Here are a few excerpts . . .

- "the *hard winter* of 1880-1881 . . . nearly quashed the city be-fore it had a chance to flourish."

- "the season's first blizzard struck in October . . . the storm raged for three days."

- "'We could not see an object ten feet from us,' wrote Eliza Wilker, a teacher."

More storms would batter the territory in the coming months and by Christmas trains had stopped running. The last train departed Pierre, heading east in December; the city would not see another until May 8, 1881. As the storms continued, precipitation accumulated throughout the long winter, and many communities measured 11 feet of snowfall. The snow formed blockades, cutting off many towns and settlements from the outside world, including 500 people in Pierre and another 300 at Fort Pierre. As the winter dragged on, food and fuel soon became scarce. The article states that "Many families were reported frozen to death and oth-ers lived wholly on turnips, some on wheat ground in a coffee mill." and that "March saw the loss of oxen and livestock and school was suspended for 30 days as wood became scarce." When spring finally arrived, record flooding occurred on the Missouri, Cheyenne, Grand, Bad, Big Sioux, Vermilion, and James Rivers.

I believe it can be said with great confidence that since 1900 there have been no winters in North America with nearly as great a deadly combination of record cold followed by record flooding as seen in the winter and spring of 1880-1881.

In the 1800s, there was nothing worse than record cold, which frequently accompanied a long winter. Thankfully, because of the changing climate, both extreme drought and intense cold have become, with very rare exceptions, something few now living have either seen or suffered.

In my study of climate, I have attempted to conduct some original research. With precipitation I have compiled, over a period of many years, the complete monthly and annual precipitation records of 51 of the oldest sites in North America, beginning in alphabetical order, with Albany, NY (1826–2024) and ending with Washington, DC (1824–2024). The Excel spreadsheet is 10,500 lines with 28 columns. Several state climatologists and others in the field have told me this effort makes up a useful contribution to knowledge.

In temperature, my most relevant work pertaining to this book has been acquiring and digitizing temperatures from the original network of stations resulting from the legislation Congress enacted in February 1870. I mentioned earlier, twenty-five stations began operation on November 1, 1870, reporting their observations via the nation's telegraph network. A major limitation was that only two stations in the West were originally part of the system. These were at Omaha, Nebraska and Cheyenne, Wyoming. But over the next few years, additional stations were quickly established and staffed. By 1875, the network was virtually national in scope and coverage.

I have digitized by hand the monthly and annual temperature records for forty of the stations, using the most balanced geographic distribution possible. To the original twenty-five stations, I could add Bismarck, Boise, Denver, Dodge City, North Platte, Portland, Salt Lake City, San Diego, Shreveport, Yankton, and others. My records are complete for all forty stations for each of the 76 years in the period 1875 through 1950. For most of the stations, I also have complete data through 2024, but more recent years data are not of interest, at least not now. The question in my mind was, *What was the temperature prior to 1895, and how does this data compare to temperatures and trends in North America through the year 1950?*

The following table summarizes the temperature data and trends for the forty-station dataset from 1875 through 1950. To the left are the coldest and warmest years, and to the right are the average temperatures for all 40 stations for sequential twenty-year intervals:

Coldest and Warmest years—40 station data; 1875-1950:				40 Station AVG Temps, by 20 years:		
YEAR	AVG TEMP	YEAR	AVG TEMP			
1875	48.67	1941	53.42	1875-1894	50.867	INCREASE
1917	49.18	1949	53.45	1895-1914	51.399	0.532
1885	49.53	1946	53.51	1915-1934	51.999	0.600
1883	49.72	1938	53.64	1931-1950	52.606	0.607
1888	49.83	1921	54.18	**TOTAL INCREASE**		**1.739**
1893	49.90	1931	54.60			

The results shown are revealing, but not surprising. 1875 was the coldest year in North America since the telegraphic reporting system began operation in November 1870. *The Maritime History of New York*, produced by the Works Progress Administration, records that the East River and Long Island Sound from Hell Gate to Sands Point froze during the winter of 1875 (WPA Writer's Project, 1941, p. 204). This was the first freezing over of these waterways since the Revolutionary War. Of the coldest years, only 1917 is more recent, and national data confirms that 1917 was the coldest year in the CONUS since 1895. And the warmest individual years are all found in the second half of the period studied. The average temperatures for 20-year increments also confirms that the initial 20 years, 1875 through 1894, were colder than 1895 through 1914 by an average of slightly over 0.5°. The final 20 years studied, 1931 through 1950, were on average a little over 1.7° warmer than the first twenty. This confirms that the warming trend in North America extends back to at least 1875. Global warming is NOT just a recent phenomenon, which began about 1990, as you may have been led to believe.

As expected, most of the coldest temperatures in individual cities over the past 150 years are from 1875 through 1894. The intense cold is found much further east and south than Montana, Manitoba, Minnesota, and the other areas already mentioned. Examples are almost too many to mention. I am a great admirer of the work of Gustavus Adolphus Hyde, (1826–1912), the longtime City Engineer of Cleveland, Ohio. Mr. Hyde (unfortunately no known relation to me) served as the longest weather observer for the Smithsonian Institution and was officially recognized as such by the government in 1905. Hyde made continuous daily weather observations in Cleveland between 1855 and 1906. He, together with the Weather Bureau, documented that the coldest years in Cleveland since 1870 were 1885, which averaged 45.59° and 1875 averaging 45.92°. In contrast, since 1900, Cleveland's three coldest years were 1917 with 46.34°, 1904 with 46.67°, and 1924 with 47.41°. Cleveland's three warmest years are 2012 at 54.03°, 2016 at 54.20°, and 2017 at 54.48°. Cleveland's temperature history is consistent with the finding that the 1800s were considerably colder than the 20th or 21st centuries. *So what?*

Well, if the reader has become convinced that warmer temperatures are a problem, then this history is bad news. But reality is the opposite. If the dead from that era could speak to us, I believe they would tell us that the cold months and years of the 1800s consistently meant hardship, suffering, economic loss, and even death. Indeed, they would be amazed and dumbfounded that the warmer temperatures recorded since 1900 are not welcomed and considered a great blessing.

Prior to 1870, there are fewer sites in North America with accepted temperature records, however, they are more than sufficient to show that the earlier years of the 1800s were even colder than anything seen in the period 1870 through 2024. I have records from 42 sites which have published monthly and annual temperatures for over 15 years, with the first complete year prior to 1860. Below are the fifteen coldest years from four of the longest sites.

St. Louis, MO		St. Paul, MN		Blue Hill, MA		Philadelphia, PA	
YEAR	AVG	YEAR	AVG	YEAR	AVG	YEAR	AVG
1856	52.37	1875	38.98	1875	42.46	1836	49.58
1857	53.00	1843	39.83	1836	43.28	1875	49.96
1836	53.20	1867	40.12	1883	43.47	1837	50.76
1978	53.23	1866	40.43	1904	43.72	1838	51.18
1838	53.29	1917	40.48	1888	43.73	1873	51.53
1875	53.42	1862	40.66	1868	43.82	1904	51.77
1843	53.58	1859	40.83	1873	43.84	1885	51.88
1849	53.72	1888	41.04	1917	43.93	1963	51.92
1933	53.74	1883	41.14	1837	43.99	1872	51.98
1945	53.74	1972	41.26	1856	44.09	1843	51.99
1917	53.74	1893	41.33	1872	44.15	1856	52.04
1883	53.78	1857	41.50	1874	44.43	1962	52.10
1847	53.79	1868	41.72	1885	44.51	1841	52.13
1869	54.07	1838	41.78	1893	44.59	1827	52.17
1855	54.08	1847	41.83	1882	44.60	1839	52.38

St. Louis, Missouri records begin in 1836, St. Paul, Minnesota in 1820, Blue Hill, Massachusetts in 1831 and Philadelphia, Pennsylvania in 1825. It is easy to see that the 1800s contain most of the coldest years. In St. Louis, for example, eleven of its 15 coldest years were prior to 1900 and of these eleven, nine are earlier than 1870. While varying in details, taken together, records from the 42 sites prove that in North America the years prior to 1870 were on average substantially colder than those since then.

The data reveals three episodes of extreme temperature before 1850, which should be summarized.

First, is the incredible cold of March 1843. As stated earlier, March 1899 was by far the coldest March in the past 126 years in North America. However, as expected, March in the earlier years of the 1800s was often much colder than 1899. In the very scholarly book, *Historic Climate*

Variability and Impacts of North America, two respected scientists, John Nielsen-Gammon and Brent McRoberts, wrote a 20-page chapter entitled "March 1843: The Most Abnormal Month Ever?" They state in the introduction to the chapter:

> Based on normalized departures of temperatures from the historic monthly mean, March 1843 may be regarded as the most anomalous month in recorded history for the central and eastern United States. In places, the average temperature for the month was more than 25° below normal, *and the expected return frequency for such an anomaly is thousands of years* [emphasis added]. The extended severe winter weather caused hardship throughout the area.

The following table gives the March 1843 average temperature for five of the longest sites, together with their next two coldest March. Note that the sites have data for from 177 years in Leavenworth to 205 years in St. Paul and Marietta, Ohio.

St. Paul, MN 205 years	Leavenworth, KS 177 years	Marietta, OH 205 years	Muscatine, IA 185 years	St. Louis, MO 188 Years
1843 4.70	1843 17.40	1843 28.20	1843 15.50	1843 26.20
1867 13.00	1867 25.80	1960 30.50	1960 22.80	1960 30.30
1899 17.10	1960 28.70	1856 32.30	1856 25.80	1906 33.30

The March 1843 temperature for St. Paul, Minnesota, was 4.26 SD below the mean for the 205-year period of record. For Leavenworth, Kansas, March 1843, the temperature was 4.07 SD below the mean. The authors of the chapter mentioned above are indeed correct—these extreme departures from normal should not have been seen since the dawn of civilization. The freezing temperatures of March 1843 extended far beyond the center of the continent. In March 1843, the temperature in Baltimore, Maryland, averaged 31.2°, the only March since 1817, which averaged below freezing. Baltimore's second coldest March averaged 33.4°.

Other record low average temperatures for March 1843 include:

- Buffalo, New York, 19.3°

- Cleveland, Ohio, 22.4°

- Detroit, Michigan, 23.8°

- Philadelphia, Pennsylvania, 30.0°

These temperatures were substantially lower than any other March. Records are available for each of these sites for between 174 to 200 years. Finally, an extremely detailed meteorological record of Natchez, Adams County, Mississippi from 1825 through 1850 was published by the state legislature in 1854. The average temperature was 46.67° during the month of March 1843. Amazingly, the coldest daily temperature recorded *during the entire year* of 1843 was 23° on March 16th. The prior year's coldest temperature on any day was 27° and in 1844, the coldest daily temperature recorded was 29° on December 17.

Only one plausible explanation for the March 1843 extreme cold is that the underlying climate in North America during the 1800s was much colder than the climate since.

The second extreme episode prior to 1850 is the record cold of December 1831. If it were not for March 1843, we would consider December 1831 to have recorded the most bizarre cold in North America in the past 200 years. There are fewer sites with temperature records dating as far back as 1831 and the only site west of Ohio is St. Paul, which averaged a record low 3.3° in December 1831. Other low average temperature records in December 1831 were:

- Buffalo, NY, 13.9°

- Blue Hill, MA, 15.7°

- Charleston, SC, 41.6°

- Cincinnati, OH, 17.3°

- New Bedford, MA, 21.0°

- New Haven, CT, 17.4°

- New York City, 22.2°

- Philadelphia, PA 25.0°

- Providence, RI, 18.2°

- Washington, DC, 25.4°

Again, each of these sites has temperature records for over 190 years and in each case the December 1831 average temperature was much lower than the second coldest December. The coldest December in the above-mentioned Natchez temperature dataset was 40.0° in 1831. The second coldest December in Natchez was 44.0° in 1825. Temperature records for New Haven, CT begin in 1778. New Haven's second coldest December was in 1790 when the temperature averaged 22.6°, or 5.2° warmer than December 1831! David L. Ludlum summarized December 1831 in his American Weather Book by saying, "1831: Coldest December ever. Erie canal closed for the entire month. New York City had a record low mean of 22°" (My note: According to Vol. 79 WWR, table pp. 891-892, the coldest Decembers in NYC since records begin in 1821 were 1831: avg. 22.2°, 1876: avg. 25.1°, and 1917: avg. 24.7°. 1917 was the coldest year in the period 1895 through 2024). December 1831 brings to mind the first quatrain of William Shakespeare's Sonnet 97: "What freezings have I felt, what dark days? What old December's bareness every where?"

The third example of extreme cold in the early 1800s is the year 1816. Any study of weather history, even just a cursory look, will quickly bring 1816 to the reader's attention. It is frequently known as "the year without summer" and at the time was colloquially called "1800 and Froze to Death." In my library, I have three excellent books on this year and the climate of the era. They are:

1. *The Last Subsistence Crisis in the Western World* by John D. Post, The Johns Hopkins University Press, 1977.

2. *Volcano Weather—The Story of the Year Without Summer* by Henry and Elizabeth Stommel, Seven Seas Press, 1983.

3. *The Year Without Summer—1816 and the Volcano That Darkened the World and Changes History* by William and Nicolas Klingman, St. Martin's Press, 2013.

Together they total nearly a thousand pages of research, thoroughly foot noted and documented. All three books present and elaborate on the premise that eruptions of the Tambora volcano on the island of Sumbawa in the Indonesian archipelago from April 5 through 12, 1815, disrupted the world's climate in 1816 and, to a lesser extent, in 1817 and 1818.

It might seem unlikely that a volcanic eruption occurring ten degrees south of the equator could affect the climate of the Northern Hemisphere halfway around the world, in North America and Europe, more than a year later. But it is accepted science that eruptions alter the climate to a greater or lesser extent. There are many examples where this hypothesis has been proven beyond any reasonable doubt. The problem is that every eruption is different in the duration, the type and amount of material ejected into the atmosphere, the location of the volcano, seasonal differences in the atmosphere's upper air circulation, and other factors.

By 1991, I owned the first two of the books mentioned above. Therefore, when Mount Pinatubo on the island of Luzon in the Philippines had a series of cataclysmic eruptions from June 12 through 16, 1991, I predicted they would affect the climate. I watched and studied subsequent climate data from the United States and Alaska. I was not therefore surprised when, in July 1993, the average temperature in Idaho was a very cold 56.2°. The second coldest July in Idaho in the 129 years 1895 through 2024 was 60.8°. July 1993 was also the coldest on record in Montana, Washington, Oregon, Nevada, and Wyoming, each by highly unusual margins. Precipitation was also just plain crazy in July 1993. Montana received 5.55 inches in July 1993, its second highest amount was 3.94 inches in 1915. North Dakota received 7.97 inches that July. Its second highest July total was 4.88 inches in 1928. Iowa received 10.45 inches in July 1993, its next highest July was 8.63 inches in 1902. Kansas, Nebraska, and South Dakota also totaled record high precipitation in July 1993 by large amounts. Missouri received 11.31 inches in September 1993, easily the greatest monthly amount in the 158 years from 1867 through 2024. Individual sites in Canada's three prairie provinces also recorded several low temperature and high precipitation records in July of that year. I calculated the standard deviations for July precipitation for Montana and North Dakota and nearly burned up my computer's central processing chip. Of course, as a mere statistician, I cannot prove that the abundantly remarkable 1993 temperature and precipitation records in North America resulted from the 1991 eruption of Mt. Pinatubo.

Therefore, I now return to 1816 . . .

The first four months of 1816 were not unusually cold. However, starting in May, temperatures were consistently below normal. The table below gives temperatures for New Haven and Salem:

New Haven, CT Period of Record 1780–1865					Salem, MA Period of Record 1786–1828				
	MAY	JUNE	JUL	AUG		MAY	JUNE	JUL	AUG
1816	52.00	60.30	65.00	67.60	1816	53.80	61.80	66.80	67.70
Normal	57.27	67.09	71.8	70.36	Normal	56.83	67.20	72.24	70.57
DEP	-5.27	-6.79	-6.80	-2.76	DEP	-3.03	-5.40	-5.44	-2.87

Williamstown, Massachusetts, is also cited in studies of 1816 since it borders New York State and is 100 miles from the Atlantic Ocean. Williamstown's May through August 1816 average temperatures were 52.8°, 60.8°, 64.6°, and 64.9° respectively. These departures from the normal were as great as in New Haven and Salem. All instrument records from that era confirm that the four primary months of the growing season in 1816 were much colder than any other year on record; resulting in widespread crop failures. The three books I reference give the details of crops that failed to ripen together with the sad and even tragic consequences. The summer temperatures throughout Europe were even colder than in

North America. This resulted in famine and disease. In Europe, death rates rose, birth rates fell, marriages postponed, and people impoverished. On the continent, the year 1816 was the worst of times. Prior famines in Europe were characterized by the saying "first dearth then plague." We see the sequence again from 1816 to 1818, when major epidemics of typhus spread across many nations.

However, it must be pointed out that the year 1816 was only one of a series of very cold years. In Salem, Massachusetts, the average temperature in 1812 was 45.26° compared to 47.10° in 1816; in fact, every year, 1812 through 1818 was unusually cold. New Haven, Connecticut, recorded eleven consecutive years, 1811 through 1821, during which annual temperatures were less than average for its period of record. Other sites show the decade 1811–1820 was abnormally cold.

It is now known that there is a long lag time from a major volcanic eruption and the first measurable effects on the earth's climate. The time lag is still being studied and debated, but almost every study concludes that a year is the minimum time for effects to be seen. The Tambora eruption could be a factor in 1816, but not 1815, or the earlier cold years.

The key lesson of the year 1816 is that the extremely cold growing season resulted in crop failures, hunger, disease, undesirable demographic changes and so on. The Tambora eruption simply made a series of cold of years worse. During the past two hundred years, summers have warmed by two to three degrees. A thinking person might conclude that because of today's much longer and warmer growing seasons, the adverse effects of future major volcanic eruptions will be much less than during the 1800s. But the Ministry of Truth will not tolerate any such independent thinkers. Everything about the warmer climate must be twisted to the negative side of the ledger. So do not believe your lying eyes—you must accept what Big Brother tells you!

Prior to 1810, there are too few sites with comprehensive instrument records to reach firm conclusions about exact temperatures in North America. There is much in the literature to show that, prior to the year 1800, winters were even colder. The principal source is the massive two-volume study written by Princeton University professor David M. Ludlum, entitled *Early American Winters 1604-1870*. The American Meteorological Society, which gives them unquestionable credibility, published the studies in 1966 and 1968. The descriptions and documents of early American winters totaling nearly 600 pages are very convincing. I summarize one example. Ludlum makes an extensive case that January 1780 was a month of record cold:

> January 1780 rated as the most persistently cold calendar month in the history of the eastern United States. At the latitude of Philadelphia the thermometer rose above freezing only once, and that for only a short time. At Hartford, Connecticut and Waltham, Massachusetts, trusted thermometers also were above the freezing mark on only one day, both at 37° on January 30th.

The account says every seaport on the North Atlantic Coast, even those not ordinarily susceptible to ice, was shut up. Philadelphia was frozen solid by December 21 and did not open for 75 days. Thomas Jefferson recounted that, "the York River near Williamsburg, Virginia froze completely and that this had not occurred previously, even in the famous freeze of 1741." Ludlum in his well-known *The American Weather Book* published in 1982 read, "January 23, 1780 was the coldest day of the coldest month in the history of the Northeast, . . . the thermometer dropped to minus 16° in New York City: harbor frozen solid for five weeks . . ."

Conditions to the north in New York were most exceptional. The entire Upper Bay of the Hudson and East Rivers froze, "so that sleighs could go back and forth from Staten Island to Manhattan and cross the narrows to Brooklyn." Both the British army and Washington's crossed at different times over the ice, "heavy loads and even cannon were dragged across the ice to Staten Island . . . 86 sleighs went from Manhattan on January 6th with provisions and ammunition." (Ludlum, 1982) Just think of the profound difference: 244 years ago, the winter ice on Long Island Sound was thick enough to support cannons weighing thousands of pounds. Contrast this with the more recent fact that until January 16, 2024, New York City had gone 701 consecutive days without even an inch of snow.

Ludlum's study begins with the winter of 1604-05 when the French attempted to establish a colony on what is now the boundary of Maine and New Brunswick. The account stated, "snow commenced early in the first week of October and continued late to the end of April . . . Thirty-five of the 79 colonists died in the bitter winter and many more barely survived." Dr. Roger F. Duncan in his massive study, *Coastal Maine—A Maritime History* (W.W. Norton & Co., New York, 1992) has a similar account of the tragic results of the abortive attempt to establish this settlement (pp. 58-59), in 1604-05. The survivors made no attempt to stay another winter in North America.

In summary, winters during the first 200 years beginning in 1604 were a series of one extreme example after another. Ludlum's chapter headings say volumes. Here are a few representative samples:

- Winthrop's Severe Winter of 1641-42

- Increase Mather's Severe Winter of 1680-81

- The Terriblest Winter of 1697-98

- Two Severe Winters Back-to-Back: 1704-05 and 1705-06

- The Great Snow of February/March 1717

- The Hard Winter of 1740-41," "The Winter of Deep Snows: 1747-48

- The Winter Siege of Boston: 1775-76

- The Long Winter of 1783-84

Today, if winter weather merely results in the cancellation of a few airline flights or ties up traffic during the rush hour, people consider it to be a major calamity.

We cannot calculate precise average temperatures at any site for the winter of 1779-80, much less any of the earlier years. Based on the conditions described, temperatures simply had to be several degrees colder than any winter since 1800, with the exceptions of 1856-57 and 1874-75. Any reasonable person would conclude that in the settled area of North America, winters were on average considerably colder from 1600 to 1800 than after 1800.

The longest and most famous temperature records known to the world are from central England. The *Central England Temperature* (CET) *Series* (a.k.a. Hadley Centre Central England Temperature or HadCET) gives monthly and annual temperature averages for 366 complete years, from January 1659 through December 2024. The average temperature in central England during this 366-year period has been 48.72°. Since 1659, the single coldest year in central England was in 1740, when the temperature averaged 44.35°. But prior to this single year, there were very long periods of cold. First, there was the sixteen-year period, 1669 through 1684, when each year saw below average temperatures. Temperature during these sixteen years averaged 47.55°. This was closely followed by the fifteen-year period 1687 through 1701, which averaged an even lower 46.89°. In central England, the coldest period of the Little Ice Age, as far as we can determine, was the 30-year period 1672 through 1701, which averaged 47.27°. In contrast, during the 20th Century the one unusually cold period in central England spanned only two years: 1962, the 57th coldest with 47.50° and 1963, the 42nd coldest with 47.34° average temperatures. Each of the coldest months in central England was also far in the past. The coldest individual month was January 1795, which averaged 26.4°. The coldest two consecutive months were January and February 1740 with 27.0° and 29.1° respectively, followed by January and February 1684, which averaged 26.6° and 30.2°. Central England's entire temperature record strongly supports the premise that, for England, the coldest temperatures of the Little Ice Age occurred well prior to 1800. Both central England and North America have been warming since the early 1800s at roughly similar rates, therefore, I believe it is reasonable to conclude that the temperatures in North America were also colder before 1800.

There are those who think that the earth's climate history for thousands of years (or even earlier) can be reconstructed by examining tree rings, Greenland's ice cores, or the ancient skeletons of diatoms, unicellular organisms, dug up from the bottom of Lake Titicaca. They are entitled to their opinion. Personally, I think those methods are no more accurate than contemplating the entrails of a freshly killed chicken. I only use instrument data and avoid anything which is not firmly data-based.

I end the examination of temperature in the 1800s by reporting what historians have said about the consequences of the extreme cold periods in Florida. As one might imagine, freezing temperatures are severely damaging there. Regrettably, there are no temperature records for Florida prior to 1825, but several datasets are available for the last three-quarters of the century.

First, the National Oceanic and Atmospheric Administration's *Preserve America Initiative* has an excellent account of the Great Florida Freeze of 1835. It states:

> The freeze of February 2-9, 1835, was the most severe of all historical freezes in the state of Florida. During this week the St. John's River was frozen, "several rods from the shore," and people were able to walk on the ice a distance from the shore . . . citrus and other fruit trees were killed to the ground, never to grow again . . . temperatures reached as low as zero degrees in both Charleston, SC and Savannah, GA and 8 F in Jacksonville . . . the state "appeared as desolate as if a fire had swept over it." "The freeze annihilated entire groves across the state, killing both mature and young trees."

The article says that the freeze ended for all-time attempts to grow citrus in southern Georgia, South Carolina, and northern Florida. In the well-known book *The Climate and Weather of Florida*, the authors include a section entitled the "Epochal Freeze of 1835." They report that the temperature in Pensacola dropped to 4°, and that ice formed in Pensacola Bay. On Sunday, February 8, 1835, the highest temperature in St. Augustine was 21°, and the city endured 56 straight hours with the temperature below freezing.

Dr. Ludlum, in his previously referenced books on North American winters, included several pages on February 1835, entitling the section "The

Great Arctic Outbreak into the South Atlantic States in February 1835." He begins by saying, "In the history of the Southern States the invasion of a cold air mass in early February 1835 provided the outstanding winter event of the century, standing without rival for degree of severity, human suffering, and economic distress." Citing no fewer than 42 sources in the literature, Ludlum describes in great detail the horrors of February 1835 in both the Carolinas, Georgia, and Florida, with shorter depictions of the deep freeze in states as far west as Louisiana. This material should be required reading for anyone who has an interest in how the climate actually was in the 1800s.

I return to Florida and provide three brief quotes, from pages 100 through 104 of Ludlum's book:

- "Dr. Baldwin, Jacksonville's longtime weatherman stated that a large area of the north of Florida was below zero."

- "Good weather records have been maintained at Jacksonville since 1829 and these confirm that the cold of 1835 has never been equaled."

- "For the record's sake, it can be stated that February 1835 was the severest ever known in northeastern Florida . . ."

But today the focus groups of the climate cultists labor long and hard to concoct reasons the modern warming of winter months is a bad thing. As expected, the media plays along, happily swallowing these artfully contrived *spins*, hook, line, and sinker.

Florida's second event was two closely spaced episodes. Initially, there was the *Big Freeze* of December 27-29, 1894. Temperatures dropped to 11° in Tallahassee, 14° in Jacksonville and 24° as far south as Fort Myers. The accounts say the damage to crops and vegetation was immense. Then January 1895 turned unseasonably warm. But six weeks after the Big Freeze of December 1894 came the real killer, the *Great Freeze* of February 1895. The historian for the *West Volusia Beacon* newspaper's article on the Great Freeze was headlined, "1895: When Florida's Beauty Disappeared." The warm January of 1895 had caused some trees to recover and sap flowed upward. But on February 7, 1895, the Great Freeze arrived in Florida with high winds and it lasted for three days. Everything was wiped out. "The February freeze finished what the December freeze had begun. Not only seedlings but older trees planted fifty years prior to that date were frozen to the core. Branches broke off like pretzels." Citrus growers reported, "over the roar of the gale, one could hear sharp cracking sounds as the trunks of citrus trees split open from the pressure of the frozen sap." The account of the freezes of December 1894 and February 1895 says, "The first freeze destroyed the wealth of a year, the second wiped out the accumulation of a lifetime."

The third, even colder, event in Florida was in February 1899, when a historic arctic cold front arrived from Canada. Professor Morton Winsberg in his book *Florida Weather* (University of Central Florida Press, 1990) said that the cold wave "was of such ferocity that it became known as the Great Arctic Outbreak of 1899." The "stupendous invasion of frigid Canadian arctic air" entered the Panhandle first and on February 12, Pensacola recorded 7°. The next day, February 13, Tallahassee officially recorded minus 2°, the only case of below zero temperature in Florida's history. In DeFuniak Springs, Florida, the temperature dropped to zero degree. In Jacksonville, on February 14, *the low for the day was 10°, and the high was 27°*. During this record outbreak of cold, the lowest temperatures ever known were recorded in twelve states throughout the nation. As examples, temperatures dropped in:

Nebraska—minus 47°

Ohio—minus 39°

Virginia—minus 29 °

Louisiana—minus 16°

Georgia—minus 17 °

Alabama—minus 24 °

On top of that, Washington, DC, received 20.5 inches of snow, a daily record. Florida's climate historians Henry, Portier, and Coyne noted dryly in their book:

> This freeze (of 1899) was not as important as the Great Freezes of 1894–1895. This can be readily understood if one realizes that the earlier freezes had ruined everything and in 1899, there was very little left to be damaged.

Florida has seen some very serious freezes since the 1800s, but none rival those described above. The most recent very cold month in Florida was December 2010, during which the temperature averaged 50.1°. Happily, there were no extremely cold individual days in the month and only a few days with strong winds. Both residents and tourists complained bitterly. Having moved from Nebraska to Florida in 2007, we thought December 2010 was still shirtsleeve weather! The average temperature for the year 2010 in Florida was 69.19°. As such, 2010 was Florida's coldest year since 1976. Everyone considered 2010 to be unpleasantly cold; as we do any year in Florida when the average temperature is less than 70°. Fortunately, because of the warming of the climate, the chance of highly destructive freezes remotely like those seen in the 1800s is now almost negligible. Even a slightly chilly year of less than 70° average temperature in Florida is now quite unlikely.

I cannot help but diverge slightly and discuss a superior article about February 1899 published in the journal, *Weather and Forecasting's* December 1988 issue, pp. 305–318, by three respected scientists. The lead author was National Aeronautics and Space Administration's Paul C. Kocin. The introduction says during the first two weeks of February 1899:

> Temperatures fell to 0 ° along the beaches of the Gulf Coast, and ice flowed from the Mississippi River into the Gulf of Mexico. All-time record minimum temperatures were established in 12 states . . . and the District of Columbia. No other cold wave has produced as many widespread low temperature records as were observed during the first half of February 1899.

In their study, the authors examined the records of 162 of the Weather Bureau's main reporting stations. I focused on Florida, but they reported than in the first week of February it was as low as 33° in Los Angeles, California, 9°, in Portland, Oregon, minus 9° in Boise, Idaho and 12° in Seattle, Washington. Then the cold moved east. By February 9, 1899, Sioux Falls, South Dakota, had recorded minus 42°, and Cincinnati, Ohio, saw minus 17°. These were among many all-time record low temperatures established from the Great Plains and Missouri to the Ohio Valley. Then the authors turned to what they called the "Main Event," the terrible five days of February 10-14, 1899. This was not just a *cold snap* of 24 to 48 hours, but five days of continuous record or near record cold. Milligan, Ohio, recorded minus 39° on February 10 and Monterey, Virginia, fell to minus 29° on the same day. On February 11, Rapid City, South Dakota, had minus 34° and Muskegon, Michigan, minus 30°. On February 12 at least 15 stations recorded all-time low temperatures including minus 45° in Scotts Bluff, Nebraska, minus 26° in Dodge City, Kansas and minus 29° in Springfield, Missouri. February 13 saw 18 stations establish record low temperatures, such as minus 16° in Minden, Louisiana, minus 20° in Lexington, Kentucky, and minus 28° in Dayton, Ohio. Six additional record lows were established on February 14, 1899, including minus 24° in Grand Rapids, Michigan.

And yet there are those who would deny that the warming of North America's climate, which has rendered anything like this and other record cold periods of the 1800s impossible, has not been a beneficial trend.

It has now been clearly shown that the 1800s were both much drier and much colder in North America than the climate the continent has experienced since 1900. But why does this matter? Which is better, a cold dry climate, or one which is warmer with greater precipitation? To provide reasonable answers to this question, data from individual states should be considered. The changes in the climate may have been beneficial for Minnesota, Montana, and North Dakota. But similar, although not identical, trends may not be welcome news in North and South Carolina.

Ninety-six examples (two for each of the contiguous states) could be provided. To illustrate simply, one for precipitation and one for temperature are given below. First, is the monthly and annual precipitation for the driest and wettest years in Minnesota from 1895 through 2024:

Monthly Precipitation—Minnesota's Driest and Wettest Years: 1895-2024

YEAR	JAN	FEB	MAR	APR	MAY	JUN	JUL	AUG	SEP	OCT	NOV	DEC	TOT
1910	0.76	0.51	0.37	1.62	1.43	1.50	2.10	2.13	2.57	0.98	0.58	0.53	15.08
2019	0.65	1.72	1.66	2.71	4.11	3.55	4.62	3.31	6.12	4.22	1.17	1.82	35.66
DIFF	(0.11)	1.21	1.29	1.09	2.68	2.05	2.52	1.18	3.55	3.24	0.59	1.29	20.58

It is assumed that the residents of Minnesota can decide if nearly 36 inches of precipitation in a year is better for them than 15 inches. They should be allowed to make this choice. Minnesota is NOT an unusual example. Its precipitation in 2019 was 138.66 percent more than in 1910. Minnesota was selected because it is NOT an extreme example. North Dakota's driest year was 1936 with 8.81 inches while in 2019 it received 24.39 inches. Thus, North Dakota's wettest year was 176.84 percent above its driest. You can bet most North Dakotans prefer 24 inches to nine.

Second, is the monthly and annual temperature data for the coldest and warmest year in Wisconsin from 1895 through 2024:

Wisconsin Monthly Temperatures—Coldest and Warmest Years: 1895-2024

YEAR	JAN	FEB	MAR	APR	MAY	JUN	JUL	AUG	SEP	OCT	NOV	DEC	AVG
1917	7.30	4.80	26.20	39.30	49.60	59.60	69.10	63.20	56.00	36.50	34.40	9.70	37.98
2012	20.80	26.60	45.60	45.10	59.60	67.10	74.80	67.10	57.70	44.80	34.40	25.10	47.39
DIFF	13.50	21.80	19.40	5.80	10.00	7.50	5.70	3.90	1.70	8.30	0.00	15.40	9.42

In Wisconsin, the first three months of 1917 were a continuation of the *five-month winter* which was all too common in that time. November 1916 averaged 30.2° and December's average temperature in Wisconsin was only 12.0°. As was typical for that era, Wisconsin endured five consecutive months of below freezing temperatures from November 1916 through March 1917. In contrast, November 2011 temperature in Wisconsin averaged 36.7° and December's average was 25.7°. Over the past century, Wisconsin's winters have become much warmer. Today below freezing average temperatures are normal only in December through February, the modern mild three-month winter.

The monthly temperature differences seen in Wisconsin between 1917 and 2012 are in fact quite representative of what has happened in the entire nation; colder months have seen by far the greatest increases, while the warmer months have experienced much smaller ones. The increase between the two Februarys was 21.8°, but six months later, the difference between the two Augusts was only 3.9°. Therefore, winters are now much shorter. The recent demise of the *long winters,* which were typical over a hundred years ago, because of the warming climate, can hardly be emphasized enough. For example, during the winter of 1916–1917 in Wyoming (which is far from being the coldest state), average temperatures in the five months November through March were 24.5°, 12.6°, 12.0°, 19.0° and 19.5°. The average temperature in Wyoming for this five-month long winter was only 17.52°. Three years later, in the winter of 1919–1920, Wyoming's April 1920 temperature averaged only 31.1°, which meant winter was a full six months long! Long winters are now extremely rare. Only the terminally obtuse will refuse to concede this important change is a major benefit of North America's warming climate.

The extent and variation of North America's temperature increase since the 1800s is illustrated in the tables below. The warming rate for each month for the contiguous 48 states is given on the left, and the monthly warming for Alaska is on the right. Note the overall warming rate in Alaska, 3.2 degrees per century, is nearly twice as great as the rate, 1.72 degrees, of the CONUS.

48 STATES	WARMING RATE PER CENTURY	ALASKA	WARMING RATE PER CENTURY
JANUARY (30.60)	2.16	JANUARY (3.0)	3.6
FEBRUARY (33.92)	3.07	FEBRUARY (5.8)	4.9
MARCH (41.82)	2.59	MARCH (11.2)	4.4
APRIL (51.27)	0.99	APRIL (23.9)	3.4
MAY (60.41)	1.07	MAY (38.4)	4.1
JUNE (68.80)	1.42	JUNE (49.6)	2.7
JULY (73.82)	1.32	JULY (53.1)	2.8
AUGUST (72.33)	1.30	AUGUST (49.8)	1.8
SEPTEMBER (65.18)	1.36	SEPTEMBER (40.8)	1.3
OCTOBER (54.23)	1.06	OCTOBER (26.2)	1.3
NOVEMBER (42.01)	1.76	NOVEMBER (12.2)	1.7
DECEMBER (33.09)	2.51	DECEMBER (4.8)	6.7
AVG	1.72	AVG (26.6)	3.2

For the contiguous states, the colder months all have warming rates of over 2 degrees per century, while the warmer months have experienced only about half as much warming. The differences in Alaska's monthly warming rates are even more dramatic. Alaska's December warming rate of 6.7 degrees per century is more than twice as rapid as its 3.2 degrees annual average. The other five colder months in Alaska also have seen much greater warming than the annual average. Obviously, the several (if not habitual) stories in the media claiming that summers have gotten much warmer are not supported by the facts, in either the 48 contiguous states or Alaska.

Another very important fact about the warming in Alaska is that it has been much more rapid in the northern parts of the state. Alaska is divided into 13 climate divisions. The northernmost division is the North Slope, which has warmed at a rate of 4.3 degrees per century. In a very revealing contrast, Alaska's southernmost division is the South Panhandle, which has warmed at only 1.6° per century. Viewed as a whole, the changes in Alaska's climate show clearly what, in fact, has happened throughout

North America. First, the overall annual temperature increases are much greater in the north than in the south.

Second, by far the greatest increase in temperature has been in the colder winter months, compared to the warmer summer months. And very substantial increases in precipitation have accompanied the increases in temperature both in Alaska and the 48 contiguous states. The table below gives warming rates per century in eight northern (colder) versus eight of the southern (warmer) states.

STATE	WARMING RATE PER CENTURY	STATE	WARMING RATE PER CENTURY
Colorado	2.2	Alabama	0.2
Maine	2.9	Arkansas	0.5
Michigan	2.6	Georgia	0.8
Minnesota	2.5	Kentucky	0.7
Montana	2.2	Louisiana	0.6
New Hampshire	2.7	Mississippi	0.3
North Dakota	2.6	Oklahoma	0.8
Wyoming	2.3	Tennessee	0.6

One must always resist the temptation to speak without permission on behalf of others, or presume to say what the citizens of a state might, or might not, prefer their climate to be. But in looking at the above temperature changes in the sixteen sample states, one cannot help but wonder what the residents think of them. Consider Arkansas, which has seen a tiny increase in temperature, only 0.5°, over the past 130 years. It can be very cold in Arkansas. Since 1895, Arkansas has recorded ten months during which the temperature averaged less than 32.0°, including 26.2° in January 1918, 26.8° in January 1940, and 27.5° as recently as January 1977. In the south, below freezing temperatures are despised. Could it not be that the citizens of Arkansas, or at least most of them, are pleased that the warming of their climate has reduced the frequency and severity of hard freezes and extended cold periods? Perhaps if the truth could be known, most people in Arkansas would like their modest warming trend to continue. In fact, they might even be pleased if a faster rate of increase was seen in the future! It is not beyond the realm of possibility that many in Arkansas would wish the temperature had increased as much as is has in Maine and New Hampshire. Of course, the climate cultists would vehemently oppose any such speculations. Mere citizens and taxpayers cannot be allowed to have any say in the matter. Their opinions or preferences are entirely immaterial. It is best that their views not be gathered or even acknowledged. The climate crazies claim they have the right to decide what temperatures are good for everyone. They expect the poor benighted and unwashed masses to follow their ex cathedra dictates mindlessly and faithfully, as if we were members of the Church of Scientology.

Near the opposite end of the above list is North Dakota, which has warmed at a rate of 2.6 degrees per century during the past 130 years. By any criteria, North Dakota has an extremely cold climate. Its average annual temperature from 1895 through 2024 has been 39.91°, the only state in the CONUS which averages less than 40°. North Dakota's summers are warm enough to be pleasant, June through August average 66.43°. Invariably, the winters are bitterly cold. Since 1895, the *warmest* winter month in North Dakota was February 1954, which averaged 29.6°. Below freezing temperatures in North Dakota can begin in September and are often recorded in May. Five (and even six) month winters are normal in North Dakota. But it is the *extreme* cold that sets North Dakota apart from other states. During the past 130 years, North Dakota recorded 31 months in which the entire state averaged below zero degrees, including two cases in which below zero average temperatures were recorded for two consecutive months. However, North Dakota has seen some definite relief from the extreme cold as the climate warmed. In the past forty years below zero average temperatures were seen only twice in January 1994, which averaged minus 1.9° and February 2019, which averaged minus 2.7°.

Earlier, I gave examples of the personal experiences with adverse climate from the writings of Thomas Barry of O'Brien County, Iowa and Laura Ingalls Wilder of Kingsbury County, South Dakota. But perhaps the best account of a family's ongoing nightmare caused by the climate is Ann Marie Low's gripping memoir entitled *Dust Bowl Diary*, 188 pages, published by the University of Nebraska Press in 1984. It would almost be unfair to just quote from this account because the entire work should be read to fully appreciate the struggles people had to endure before the climate turned for the better. Low's (née Riebe) account is about life on their farm in rural Stutsman County in southeastern North Dakota. She tells of her family's life from 1927, "the last good year in North Dakota" in her opinion, to 1937. Her diary ends that summer when she is 25 years old. She has finished her third year as a high school teacher in Medora, a small town in the North Dakota Badlands. Nearly all the money she earned has was given to her desperate family to keep them from losing the farm. She wrote in June 1937:

> I feel trapped in the same round all over again . . . all I could spare, including almost all my last pay check went to Mama and Bud. I scarcely have enough money for bus fare home—to just an everlasting round of work (on the farm) in the Stony Brooke country that has been ruined. This is a round that will go on forever. At least it will go on until my youth is gone. Somehow, I have got to get out!

I cannot resist the temptation to include a few more quotations from Low's unique contribution to climate history . . .

- Grandpa's high hopes and hard work (in the Dakota Territory) met with continual discouragement. The disaster of summer droughts in the 1880s was coupled with bitterly cold winters. (p. 10)

- Dad said the blizzard of November 1929 reminded him of the winter of 1896-97 when rain in October turned into a blizzard. Grandpa killed the best horse he ever rode getting home. Coal had not yet been shipped into the state . . . Grandma burned the furniture and grain to keep from freezing . . . The snow kept coming: winter lasted until May. Fences and houses were buried under deep drifts and the coulees were level with the hills. (p. 32)

- This is the worst winter I ever saw. There was one blizzard after another, and for six weeks the warmest day has been 10 below zero. From there is has ranged down to 40 below . . . I hear the CCC Camp (the federal government's make-work program) is having an awful time getting food and fuel. In this country people stock up on such things in the fall, but not these government geniuses. A couple of the boys have died. The camp doctor could not or would not care for them . . . Since last Sunday they have smashed up two tractors and six trucks trying to get fuel to the camp. Cap (a neighbor a few miles away) is snowed in alone on the farm . . . He says the drifts in the yard are 18 feet deep, so he cannot get a horse out, but occasionally walks to town on top of the drifts. (p. 134)

These are only representative examples. Other longer ones could have been provided. Including an extended heartbreaking episode where, because of winter storms, the cattle and hogs could not be shipped to market, food and forage were eventually exhausted, and the poor animals starved. In the end, they were simply shot to put a stop to their suffering. And yet, there are many who believe that the warmer and wetter climate of today is worse than that of decades ago. Much worse! The appalling ignorance of this attitude is amazing.

Given North Dakota's extensive history with an adverse climate, one might wonder what North Dakotans feel about their warmer temperatures, not to mention the terrific increase in precipitation that has accompanied the warming. As usual, it is worthwhile to give some attention to the details. While the temperature for the state has been warming at a rate of 2.6 degrees per century, this varies among the nine climate divisions. Climate Division 1 (Northwest) the coldest in the state has been warming faster at 2.8° per century, while Climate Division 9 (Southeast) the warmest, has warmed at 2.2° per century. This is what would be expected. The greatest warming is consistently found in the coldest areas. And as would also be expected, temperatures in North Dakota have warmed the most in the coldest months. January and February have warmed at rates of 5.5 and 6.0 degrees per century, while July and August have warmed at only

1.2° and 1.9° per century. The greatest increases in temperature have been in January, Climate Division 2 (North Central) which has warmed at a rapid rate of 6.2 degrees per century. In Climate Division 1 (Northwest), February has warmed at a rate of 6.5 degrees per century! If informed of this, I would bet the secular residents would thank their lucky stars for this change. But the old-fashioned German Lutherans in North Dakota would be much more apt to spontaneously break into singing the doxology, "Praise God from whom all blessings flow!" By happy coincidence, December 2023 was the warmest December in North Dakota's history, averaging 26.7°, surpassing the 25.4° of December 1939 by an amazing 1.3°. But back to the point, do the people who live in North Dakota believe this warming is harmful or beneficial? Do they want it to stop warming or would they, in fact, welcome more warming in the future? Do North Dakotans even have a right to express their opinion? Or should they just keep quiet and save their breath because the climate cultists have seized control of the government? These are not just rhetorical questions. Someday, the climate crazies may wake up and find that they have ignored the views and welfare of ordinary people for too long and that the hod carriers who really make our country work have risen and demand to be heard!

The final data relating to temperature concerns the relationship between warm, cold, and mortality. To put the facts in simple terms, there are many more deaths in cold months than during warm months. The following table gives the average death rates per day in the United States during the six years 2014 through 2019. All six of these years were examples of normal pre-COVID mortality rates.

Deaths in the USA	TOTAL DEATHS	DEATHS PER DAY
July 2014–2019	1,322,206	7,108.63
August 2014–2019	1,315,749	7,073.92
December 2014–2019	1,490,244	8,012.06
January 2014–2019	1,561,701	8,396.24

The data is irrefutable. Deaths in cold months are over 15 percent higher than in warm months. This relationship, with very minor variations either way, extends back in time to at least the year 1900, for which the first annual mortality records are available. The year 1918 is the one exception to this rule. During the Great Influenza of 1918, deaths peaked in October and November.

Death data since the COVID pandemic struck is even more remarkable. Mortality rates in the cold and warm months during the first two years of COVID are astonishing:

Deaths in the USA	TOTAL DEATHS	DEATHS PER DAY
December 2020	366,568	11,824.77
January 2021	372,916	12,029.55
August 2020	276,731	8,926.81
July 2021	257,328	8,300.90

During the COVID years of 2020 and 2021, deaths per day were 38 percent higher in the cold months of December and January compared to July and August. Deaths exceeded 12,000 per day in January 2021. Prior to COVID, deaths above 9,000 per day in the United States had been recorded only once, in January 2018, when deaths averaged 9,250 per day. Final month-by-month mortality data is not yet available for 2022, but the provisional data shows that the pattern seen in 2020 and 2021 was unchanged. During 2022, the daily death rate during the cold months was again about 40 percent higher than deaths per day during the warmer months.

This is a fact, not a theory. In *normal* years, the average daily death rate is over 15 percent higher in cold months than in warm months. If COVID is a reliable example, the death rate during outbreaks of deadly infectious diseases will be much greater in cold months in relative terms. A reasonable person might therefore wonder why the climate cultists consider the warming of winter months to be such an unmitigated disaster.

To conclude, the examination of temperature, it is beneficial to put the climate of the 1800s (as well as today's, for that matter) into the context of the Little Ice Age. I have many books and articles about this subject. While there is not an unanimous consensus, a majority of scientists and historians put the beginning of the Little Ice Age in about the year 1300. As such, it follows another fluctuation of the world's climate known as the Medieval Warm Period. This beneficial epoch lasted, with even greater uncertainty as to its beginning and end, from about 800 or 900, until ca. 1300. For example, the well-known author Ken Follett, in his book about the construction of cathedrals in Europe, states the period was from 950 to 1250. However, there is some very compelling evidence that the cooling climate began well before the year 1300.

The best and most scholarly book on the Little Ice Age is a graduate school level college textbook oddly entitled, *The Little Ice Age* by Dr. Jean M. Grove, (xxii and 496 pages), published by Methuen–London and New York. It is obscenely expensive, but I finally broke down and purchased a copy. In the introduction, Dr. Grove talks about the Medieval Warm Period and the beginning of the Little Ice Age:

> For several hundred years climatic conditions had been kind; there were few poor harvests and famines were infrequent. The pack ice in the Arctic lay far to the north and long sea voyages could be made in the small craft then in use . . . Icelanders made their first trip to Greenland in about AD 982 . . . Grain was grown in Iceland and even in Greenland; in mainland Europe vinelands were in production 55 km north of their present limits . . . The beneficent times came to an end, Sea ice made the passages between Norway, Iceland and Greenland more difficult *after AD 1200* (emphasis supplied) and the last report of a voyage to Greenland was in 1347. Life in Greenland became harder; the people were cut off from Iceland and eventually disappeared from history . . .

Dr. Brian Fagan, in his more readable book, *The Little Ice Age* confirms the same story, "Tree rings and ice cores tell us that the Little Ice Age cooling began in Greenland and the Arctic in about 1200." (p. xvi) plus ". . . we now know that the first glacial advances began around Greenland in the early thirteenth century, while countries to the south were still basking in warm summers and settled weather," (p. 49).

Finally, there is the very evocative history of Iceland entitled *Golden Iceland* by the famous French historian Samivel. The work was translated into English by Magnus Magnusson and distributed in the United States by J. B. Lippincott Company, Philadelphia and New York. This work also deals extensively with the settlements of Greenland and their tragic end. From pp. 86–87:

> In the twelfth and thirteenth centuries the people (of Greenland) moved around a great deal in the good season and even in the bad . . . It was then that the demons of frost began to kill them off; imperceptibly . . . It was the first warning sign of one of the waves of glaciation which succeed one another on the surface of the globe to a rhythm and for reasons still not fully understood . . . The deterioration of the climate was scarcely perceptible at first . . . frosts late in the spring . . . ponds which froze around midnight up in the mountains right in the middle of August . . . The Eskimos arrived too, this migration was doubtless caused by the gradual lowering of the temperature which drove the seals toward the south, and the Eskimos followed the seals. During this time the pitiless tide of cold moved down toward the coasts, gradually engulfing a country that was once green; the frost devoured the pastures, and the herbage could not ripen in the shortening summers. Each year more ground had to be abandoned, one hillside surrendered, then another, and there was no fodder for winter. Then the infernal cycle started speeding up. Cattle had to be killed for food. When fifty years earlier there had been twenty cows in the byre, now there were only ten, or even fewer. Famine began to knock at the doors with the winter blizzards, bringing its emaciated train of physical misery and disease.

For some years after 1327, there had been no communication at all with the settlement on the west coast of Greenland. Finally, about 1340, an expedition made it to the site . . . "Ivar Bardarson found not a living soul in the Western Settlement, nothing but 'the gaping mouths of doors' and a few beasts wandering disconsolately about the empty countryside."

The Little Ice Age certainly had not arrived in Europe or Asia by the year 1300. But I state the case that in the most northern latitudes the warmer temperatures of the Medieval Warm Period had peaked, and it had turned colder around 1200. I also present the view that the coldest years of the Little Ice Age occurred about 500 years later, around 1700.

To support this premise, I cite the work *Ice Ages: Solving the Mystery* by John and Katherine Imbire, Harvard University, Cambridge, MA. On page 183, they write the Little Ice Age reached its coldest "about A. D. 1700 and was the last of five similar Holocene events . . ." and from page 184, ". . . the warming effect of the present cycle which began to be felt about the year 1700 . . ." The CET series certainly confirms this idea. The coldest fifteen-year period of the Little Ice Age was 1687 through 1701 and the coldest 30 consecutive years in central England was 1672 through 1701.

It is clear that the Little Ice Age was only the most recent of several temperature cycles the earth has seen over the past 10,000 years. As an example, just prior to the Little Ice Age, the earth saw the Medieval Warm Period. Without doubt the length of the cycles has varied, and the date of their beginnings and ending, as well as their highest and lowest temperatures, become more indefinite the further into history we retreat. There is universal agreement on one aspect of these climate oscillations—the world cools beginning the at poles and the cold, over the years, decades, and even centuries progresses toward the equator. At some point the cold's relentless march halts and after a period of perilous equilibrium, warmth, imperceptibly at first, returns. Eventually, the cold is pushed back toward its natural home at the poles. I will return to this idea below.

To provoke thought, consider this: If the cooling of the Little Ice Age began about the year 1200 and *peaked* (in a negative sense) about 1700, then the cooling cycle spanned about 500 years. If the subsequent warming *rebound* was to be of equal length, that would mean the earth would gradually warm from about 1700 to about 2200. So, as of 2025, the earth would be about 325 years into the warming cycle with about 175 years of additional warming remaining. I am sure this reasoning, even as speculation, just caused many of the climate cultist's heads to explode. Facts like the Little Ice Age and indeed all talk of climate cycles make them very uncomfortable because it threatens their new-age like religion. According to the climate crazies' doctrine, ALL warming is caused by human activity! Not a single degree, or even a tenth of a degree of warming can possibly be because of natural causes! This is despite the fact science has shown natural causes (although they are not well understood) have worked to change the climate countless times throughout the earth's history. The irrefutable science which has confirmed many climate cycles be dammed!

To return to the idea that the climate is engaged in an eternal struggle between cold and warm, please indulge me for a minute. Imagine that you have never heard of either climate change or the Little Ice Age. Let us further assume that you are familiar with arithmetic and the concept of averages and can analyze data as well as any other intelligent adult. You are presented with the monthly and annual temperature data for a long-term site in North America and are asked to determine what, if anything, has been happening to the temperature over the past 175 to 200 years. You are asked to pay particular attention to 30-year intervals and their averages, because you are told, periods of less than 30 years are less reliable. So, now you examine the temperature data for St. Paul, Minnesota, which begins in October 1819 and end with December 2024. The *period of record* is therefore 205 years and three months. After just a few minutes of analysis, you see it was much colder in the 1800s. In effect, the Little Ice Age has announced itself to you; it virtually leaps off the spreadsheet, demanding to be recognized as the primary feature of over 200 years of temperature history. In St. Paul, the Little Ice Age *peaked* in the 30-year period 1847 through 1876, during which the temperature averaged 42.62°. The climax was in 1875, the coldest of the 204 years, which averaged only 38.98°. The next year, 1876, saw the beginning of a warming trend. The warming sped up at an amazing rate over the next two or three decades. In the subsequent 30-year period, 1877 through 1906, the temperature in St. Paul average 44.22°, an incredible increase of 1.6°! Since 1906, the temperature in St. Paul continued to increase, although there were some minor and temporary pauses. The warmest 30 years in St. Paul were the most recent, 1994 through 2023, which averaged 47.00°. Included in this 30-years, as expected, was the single warmest year, 2012, which averaged an oppressively hot 50.78°. This was 11.81° warmer than during 1875!

As usual, the annual averages do not really tell how cold the 1800s were in St. Paul and how the hideous cold has been gradually defeated by the angelic warm. Average temperatures in December, 1822 and 1831, was 3.3°, December 2023's was 34.3°! January and February 1875 averaged below zero degree at minus 2.6° and minus 2.3°. November 1838 temperature averaged 20.5°, November 1896 21.9° and November 1880 22.1°. April 1857 averaged only 32.4°, and April is supposed to be the first real month of spring. The notorious five-month winters of the Little Ice Age were common in St. Paul. November through March 1874-1875 averaged only 13.36°, which makes one wonder how people even survived. Six more November through March winters in the 1800s averaged less than 16.0°, far colder than any recorded since 1900.

The changes in the *monthly* temperature averages tell the complete story of how the Little Ice Age has been vanquished. The *annual* temperature average has increased by 4.38°, from the 42.62° of 1847–1876 to the 47.00° average of 1994–2023. Consider the monthly increases in the cold five months and the three relative warm months in St. Paul:

	AVG 1847-1876	AVG 1994-2023	INCREASE F
NOV	30.43	35.45	5.02
DEC	14.97	22.16	7.19
JAN	10.65	16.08	5.43
FEB	15.48	19.65	4.17
MAR	26.39	33.24	6.85
JUNE	67.47	70.19	2.72
JULY	71.95	74.70	2.75
AUG	68.11	72.05	3.94

Here again is proof, if any more is needed, that the warming of the climate has been concentrated in colder months, with much less warming occurring in the summer.

The example of St. Paul can be seen in every one of the longest-term temperature datasets found in North America, which lie north of the 35th Parallel. It is obvious in Albany, New York, Baltimore, Maryland, Blue Hill, Massachusetts, Cleveland, Ohio, Dubuque, Iowa, Leavenworth, Kansas, New Haven, Connecticut, St. Louis, Missouri, Peoria, Illinois, Philadelphia, Pennsylvania, Toronto, Ontario, and Washington, DC, just to name a few. It is most obvious and greatest in the sites furthest from the Atlantic Ocean, but is clearly present and identifiable, even in the coastal cities. The Little Ice Age peaked in the mid-to-late 1800s, varying by a decade or two from site to site. The strong warming trend which continues unabated today had started almost everywhere by the 1880s, or in some cases even earlier.

But . . . there is a problem.

Note I said the Little Ice Age and the subsequent warming trends could be clearly identified in sites *north of the 35th parallel.* However, in the southern United States, I cannot find solid evidence, much less proof, that the Little Ice Age even visited the area. The problem is two-fold. First, there are only a few good sites in the South with long-term temperature data from the early 1800s which extend through to the end of the 19th Century. Second, in the few sites which have data, the Little Ice Age just does not show up! There is a form of *Test Takers Bias* by which if a person believes the data should reveal something, if you try hard enough, you will eventually find the results you want! This is the approach I took in examining the temperatures datasets from locations in the South. The Little Ice Age must be hiding somewhere in the data! But, in the end, I must admit I was defeated.

Over the past decades, I have gathered data from 44 long-term temperature sites in North America from every possible published source. My criteria for this study are that a site must have complete temperature data for at least fifteen years and at least one year must be prior to 1860. These are quite liberal criteria. Only six of the 44 sites are in the South. The State of Ohio alone has seven sites which easily exceed both criteria! Below, I summarize the six southern sites which have useful temperature data:

City and State	Number of Years	Latitude	1st Year POR
Charleston, SC	128	32.47 N	1823
Jacksonville, FL	68	30.20 N	1830
Key West, FL	85	24.33 N	1830
Tampa, FL	78	27.57 N	1825
Natchez, MS	24	31.33 N	1825
Washington, AR	20	33.40 N	1840

The last two sites listed can be dealt with in a few sentences. The first is Natchez, Mississippi. The Mississippi state government published data in 1854. It has data for 24 years, 1825 through 1850, with some of 1848 and all of 1849 missing. It is interesting because it confirms the extreme cold mentioned earlier in December 1831 and March 1843 extended deep into the South. Average temperature in December 1831 was 40°. The next coldest in the series is 44° and the warmest December averaged 59°! In March 1843, the temperature was even more startling, averaging only 46.7°. Followed by the next coldest March in 1835, which was 55.5°. The warmest March in the series was 69.3° in 1842. This again shows that March 1843 was, in a relative sense, the coldest month in North America since 1820 or even earlier. Beyond this, the temperature data shows no trend and adds very little. The coldest year was 1831 with 62.92°, while the warmest year was five years earlier, 1826, which averaged 69.25°.

Washington, Hempstead County, in southern Arkansas, has tempera-ture data for 20 years from 1840 through 1859. It was incredibly cold in March 1843; the temperature averaged only 35.28°. The second coldest March was 1847, which averaged 46.9°, over ten degrees warmer! March 1849 was the warmest, averaging 62.68°. The coldest month was January 1856, which averaged 33.97°. January 1856 was also the coldest month ever seen in Leavenworth, KS, as well as some other sites north of Arkansas. Beyond the data for these months, the dataset simply is not long enough to contribute further.

In complete contrast, climate records, both of temperature and precipitation, for Charleston, South Carolina are among the longest and most homogeneous of any site in North America. Surely the Little Ice Age will be apparent in Charleston's records. The well-known series of books *World Weather Records*, published by the Smithsonian Institution, has Charleston's data from inception through 1940, and the continuation of the series published by the Department of Commerce has data for 1941 through 1950. Good data, with no missing months or years, is available for 1823 through 1950. During these 128 years, the coldest year averaged 63.62° and the warmest 71.12°. The range of 7.50° is quite large for a site in the southern United States. The first warning that Charleston's data will not provide the answers we seek is the fact that the coldest year was 1901 and the warmest 1828! In fact, the four warmest years are 1828, 1830, 1834, and 1860. The four coldest years are 1901, 1886, 1917, and 1940. Even the year 1886 is ten or more years after the coldest annual temperatures are expected. Using the more scientific method of examining average temperatures over 30-year intervals, there were no unusually cold 30-year periods in the 1800s. It is extremely odd, but the general trend of Charleston's temperature began with amazingly warm temperatures from 1823 through 1854. Then, very gradual and uneven cooling began, which lasted until 1920. Finally, in 1921, a very gradual and uneven warming trend began in Charleston. But none of these trends were dramatic or substantial or show major temperature changes as found in other long-term North American sites.

Charleston saw some unusually cold months in the 1800s. The three coldest months were January 1871, which averaged 38.2°, followed by January 1856 with 39.4° and January 1940 with 39.6°. The coldest March, as expected, was 1843, which averaged 48.0°, followed by 1915 with 49.1°. Note, however, this difference is only 1.1°. Still, it adds evidence that the great cold of March 1843 covered all the eastern United States. The three months January through March 1856 averaged only 46.67°, over 1.5 degrees colder than any similar three months in the 128-year period. But, a few very cold months does not a Little Ice Age make!

However, it must also be noted that each of the twenty warmest months in Charleston from 1823 through 1950 was recorded during the 1800s. July 1838 was the hottest month averaging 86.7°, followed by August 1836 with 86.3°. Frankly, I would have been delighted to find strong (or even meager) evidence of the Little Ice Age in Charleston's temperature data. But the fact is, none is there.

There is also no evidence of the Little Ice Age in the final three sites in the south: Jacksonville, Key West, and Tampa, Florida. As in Charleston, the coldest year at each site was 1901. This makes sense because 1901 was substantially the coldest year in Florida in its 134 years of records, 1891 through 2024. In the entire period of record for the three sites, beginning in either 1825 or 1830, there is very little *range* or difference between the coldest and warmest years. Jacksonville has the greatest range, but only 4.8° between the coldest, 67.0° in 1901, to the warmest, 71.9° in 1830. Monthly data from the three Florida sites is equally boring. The coldest month by over two degrees was in Jacksonville when it averaged 45.5°— not during the 1800s, but in January 1940!

Besides the six southern sites mentioned above, in the West there are three sites which have temperature records beginning prior to 1860: Santa Fe, New Mexico and San Francisco and San Diego, California. Santa Fe's data begins in 1849. Unfortunately, each site has data missing in several years. Santa Fe has eight complete years prior to 1860, San Francisco six complete years and San Diego nine complete years. Beginning with the year 1861, there are almost complete temperature records for all three sites. Be this as it may, we find little evidence for the Little Ice Age in the temperature data of the three sites. None of the sites has a period even as brief as five years in the 1800s, which was unusually cold compared to temperatures in the period 1900 through 1950. Monthly temperature data also reveals no secrets. Well . . . there was ONE rather unusual period in San Francisco. In San Francisco, a month where the temperature averages less than 50.0°, is relatively uncommon. The coldest month in San Francisco's record was January 1937, which averaged 43.2°. The average temperature in December 1879 was 44.6°, which was the coldest December on record by 2.0°. January 1880 averaged 46.8°, the 16th coldest January. February 1880 averaged 47.3 °, which is tied for the second coldest. Finally, March 1880 averaged 48.2°, which was the second coldest March—only 1897 was slightly colder with 48.0°. This four-month cold spell in San Francisco was much colder than any similar period since then. Was San Francisco's cold winter of 1879-1880 evidence of the Little Ice Age? Hardly. I maintain that one four-month episode, however strange, does not prove much of anything.

There is simply no evidence of the Little Ice Age in the temperature data in any of the nine sites lying near or south of the 35th parallel in North America. Therefore, I suggest the following theory: The Little Ice Age was in a sense like the Ice Ages of old in that there was a point or line beyond which its effects were much less or nil. Regrettably, the data does not determine exactly where this line is (or might be). But for convenience, I note that the northern borders of North Carolina, Tennessee, Arkansas, Oklahoma, New Mexico, and Arizona form a nearly straight line, varying only slightly from 36.3° to 37.0° N. This line extends for 1500 miles across almost all the United States. I pose, as food for thought, that the Little Ice Age in North America did not extend south of this line, with one prominent exception. The Great Arctic historic cold fronts which invaded the United States several times during the 1800s from Canada as horrifying Alberta Clippers, Saskatchewan Screamers, and Manitoba Maulers did not hesitate to go beyond all state lines. These masses of polar air hit the South extremely hard, causing immense suffering and damage, as has already been described. The final, and perhaps most extreme, example of an invasion of Canadian cold occurred in early February 1899. It has been extensively studied and written about in more than a dozen articles and scientific papers. Not only did the cold of February 1899 inundate the southern states, it tore through the Florida Keys, stunning Key West with the coldest temperatures on record. It then continued across the Gulf of Mexico to Cuba, wreaking havoc with high winds in Havana and elsewhere. Before dying, it even reached Jamaica, where it was "strongly felt" in Kingston, the capital city.

However, in no case did the memorable temper tantrums and petulant outbursts of the Little Ice Age cause the extreme cold in the south to stay for longer than a week. In most instances, the record cold associated with these events lasted for only two to four days.

I cannot help briefly returning to the February 1899 event. In February 1999, the National Weather Service issued an article observing the Centennial of this *Benchmark Cold Wave*. The article described it as "The Mother of all Cold Waves," stating that, among other things, it "paralyzed the Eastern Seaboard" and "brought ice to the Gulf of Mexico." The damage was extremely widespread . . . "in Chicago, the freeze penetrated into the ground up to five feet, causing great damage to water, gas, and sewer pipes." The list of severe consequences goes on and on. Every person who wishes to know the truth about what the climate did to the nation in 1899 and earlier in our history would benefit from reading this piece. The suffering was not limited to humanity. In Tennessee the cold caused "nearly the complete extinction of the bluebird population." In Virginia, the quail population was nearly wiped out. The article lists eighteen species of birds that were similarly affected. The cold wave resulted in about 100 human deaths, including the deaths of mail carriers in two towns in New York State. Crops and orchards were ruined in Georgia, and as far away as Washington state, most of the winter wheat crop was destroyed. One article gives an extensive analysis of the immense loss of livestock, including sheep, cattle, horses, and pigs. Traffic was brought to a halt in all parts of the country, barge traffic was brought to a complete standstill, railroads were delayed or paralyzed, and steamships, freighters, and liners were delayed. The record cold wave deserves every article and study that has been written about it. Yet the event's existence has evaporated from the national consciousness. This is in no small part because of the efforts of the climate cultists who for decades have studiously avoided acknowledging any of the terrors, horrors, and destruction the climate of the 1800s brought to North America.

It is necessary to give some specific attention to the temperature changes in Canada, according to its historical instrument records. Climate data for Canada is much more limited than for the United States. Only one site,

Toronto, has continuous monthly and annual climate records from before 1850. And only two other sites, Montreal and Winnipeg, have similar continuous data that begins prior to 1875. St. John's, Newfoundland, data begins in 1872 but is missing for some months and even entire years. However, where data is available for specific sites in Canada, it is just as accurate and reliable as from sites in the United States. The problem is, the data available from Canada is just a small fraction of that in the USA.

Complete climate data for Canada has only been produced beginning for the year 1948. This is probably because Newfoundland and Labrador were not part of Canada until after World War II. Canada now has 76 years, 1948–2023, of complete temperature data available. But Canada's data has limitations. The main temperature data is published for each calendar quarter, January through March, etc. No readily available monthly reports are published for Canada and there is no good *interactive* dataset open to the public as in the United States. If someone in the United States, for example, wishes to study the temperature changes of June through August (or any other odd sequence of months) in the northern third of Iowa, (or any other idiosyncratic area), from 1901 through 2000, (or any other period of two or more years since 1895), they can generate this data, both in table and graph form, and save to their computer in just a couple of minutes. Canada's quarterly temperature reports are eventually followed (several months later) by a rather meager annual summary.

It is awkward and frankly nonsensical that Canada's temperature analysis uses the 30 years 1961 through 1990 as the "base reference period." As such, Canada presents its quarterly and annual changes or deviations as departures from this base. The problem is, the 30 years 1961 through 1990 were unusually cold and thus they do not make up a proper sample from which to judge temperature changes and trends. Of this 30-year period, only 1981 and 1987 were unusually warm, being the 7th and 13th warmest since 1948. But the 30 years, 1961 through 1990, contain most of Canada's coldest years since 1948; 76th (the coldest) the 74th, 73rd, 71st, 70th 68th, the 66th coldest and so on. Of the 30 years in Canada's strange 1961 through 1990 base, only five were slightly warmer than average and

25 were colder. The bottom line is by using a very cold base period, the temperature increases Canada reports are considerably greater than what would be shown if a neutral base were used. It is safe to say than no reputable scientist or statistician today would dare to select a base period that is skewed one way or the other if they ever hoped to get a scholarly paper published in a respected journal.

Finally, Canada presents its climate data for *eleven climate regions*. However, none of the fanciful regions match up nicely with the boundaries of its provinces or any other geographic *metes and bounds* one might expect or find highly useful. In the United States, all climate data is available for 48 states, and 344 climate divisions within the states. Plus, if one wishes to look at custom multi-state, regional climate areas in the United States, such as the West or Northeast, these can be created and called up with just a few keystrokes.

Be all these limitations as they may, Canada's temperature trend since 1948 is as follows. Temperature in Canada has increased by 2.0°C over the past 77 years when compared to its somewhat problematic 1961–1990 base period. This is a greater average temperature increase than that seen across the northern tier of states such as Montana, North Dakota, Minnesota, Maine, etc. which border Canada. This is as expected because the temperature in North Dakota is increasing faster than in South Dakota, and so on. Similarly, temperature in the three northern climate divisions of North Dakota is increasing faster than in the state's three southern climate divisions. Within Canada's awkward climate regions, it is clear than the greatest temperature increase is in the north. In Canada's three southernmost regions, Atlantic, Great Lakes, and Pacific coast, the temperature has increased at 1.2°C, 1.4°C, and 1.6°C, respectively. In contrast, the temperature in three very large northern climate regions, Yukon, Mackenzie, and Arctic, has increased by 2.7°C, 2.8°C, and 2.6°C. Canada's south to north temperature increases are quite similar to those seen throughout the United States, except more so. Canada's temperature changes since 1948 constitute a prime example of Global Warming—on steroids!

To illustrate the amazing warming that has occurred in Canada, it is useful to look at the changes seen at a specific site. Winnipeg, Manitoba, serves this purpose well. Below are the monthly and annual temperatures in Winnipeg for two years. The year 1883 was the coldest since Winnipeg's records began in 1873. The year 1883 is compared below to temperatures recorded in 1987, which, as I pointed out above, was the 13th warmest year in Canada's period of record.

YEAR	JAN	FEB	MAR	APR	MAY	JUN	JUL	AUG	SEP	OCT	NOV	DEC	AVG
1883	-16.2	-6.0	6.5	32.8	45.6	61.2	62.3	61.2	51.4	36.4	14.6	-1.8	29.0
1987	10.9	20.7	23.5	48.0	58.6	66.2	68.0	63.1	57.4	38.3	30.7	17.4	41.9
INC	27.1	26.7	17.0	15.2	13.0	5.0	5.7	1.9	6.0	1.9	16.1	19.2	12.9

The temperature increase seen in Winnipeg over the 105-year period is virtually a microcosm for the northern United States and Canada. First, the annual increase of 12.9 degrees is immense. Winnipeg no longer has entire years with an average temperature below 32.0°. There were eight exceptionally cold years in Winnipeg from 1873 to 1899 when the temperature averaged below freezing, but only one since 1900; 1950, which averaged 31.82°. In addition, the beneficial warming trend mirrors that seen elsewhere. The warming of the cold winter months is several times greater than the increase seen in the warmer months—27.1 degrees warmer in January versus only 1.9 degrees in August, as extreme examples. Long gone in Winnipeg are the frigid temperatures where the thermometer barely registers above zero for an entire month. In the 1800s, there were many years when the average temperature was below zero for two, or even three consecutive months. Not seen in Winnipeg for more than a century were years when even the average temperature in April was incredibly cold: 1893—26.9°, 1874—27.1°, and 1907—28.2°. In these cases, winter lasted for six months, November through April. November 1873 temperature averaged only 12.5° and the average temperature in Winnipeg during the six months Nov. 1873 through April 1874 was only 8.27°. But it was even colder in the six months of 1874-75, which averaged 6.13°, and in 1892-93 when November through April averaged only 5.02°! Brutal cold winters of five months in Winnipeg during the

1800s are too common to list. In the five-month winter of November 1886 through March 1887, the temperature in Winnipeg actually averaged slightly below zero at minus 0.22°.

One cannot help but wonder what the residents of Winnipeg, and indeed citizens of the three prairie provinces from Alberta to Manitoba, think of today's warmer (and wetter) climate compared to their dry and frigid past. One would be hard put to explain in simple declarative sentences why the twin changes of greater precipitation and warmer temperatures are anything but highly beneficial. However, you can bet that the climate crazies can conjure up long and elaborate arguments why this inconvenient truth must be rejected. But they needn't worry or get all het up. The climate cultists completely dominate Canada's leaders in Ottawa. What may be good for the prairie provinces, or if their people wish the climate trends of the past 150 years to continue, matters not a bit to those in power.

I am prepared to be mocked for the following analogy. I believe the climate of the world, with its continuous cycles, episodic changes, oscillations, and periodicities, can be likened to an endless war between angels and demons (with apologies to author Dan Brown). In this titanic struggle, there are two demons who continuously try to turn the climate against both humans and all higher life forms. The Chief Demon is Cold. Cold is assisted by his clever and destructive partner Drought. Working just as diligently to improve the climate for the benefit of humanity and warm-blooded animals are two angels. The Chief Angel is Warmth. Warmth is assisted by his wonderful healing partner, Precipitation, which for convenience I will just call Rain. During the Ice Ages, the demons were at the height of their power, reigning victorious over most of the earth. Throughout the Ice Ages most of the earth, because of the triumph of Cold and Drought, was unfit to support any type of civilization or higher life forms. But Warmth and Rain were never completely defeated. After tens of thousands of years, they finally turned the tide; thawed the earth, provided water, and created a beneficial climate. Therefore, we now have the warm and wet conditions prevalent over the past several thousand years. These conditions have allowed human civilization to develop and prosper, the earth to be explored, and the world's economies to grow until the modern climate now supports a population estimated by the United Nations to be over 8.2 billion souls as of January 2025.

Within the past several thousand years, the angels and demons have fought several battles to preserve or degrade our present warm and wet climate. Cold and Drought attacked most recently from 1200 to 1300 and successfully brought the 500-year Little Ice Age down on the earth. This followed the 300 to 400-year beneficial time, from about 900 to 1300, known as the Medieval Warm Period (MWP). Prior to the MWP, the climate of the Dark Ages is less well-known, but it was definitely cooler than during the MWP. One theory, which is well-supported, is that there was a sixth-century climate catastrophe during the heart of the Dark Ages which engulfed the entire world. It centered on the years 535-536 when, evidence shows, the climate of the earth spun out of control and remained horrible for the next two or three decades. There was drought and famine everywhere. I commend this story, which one historian called "The Winepress of the Wrath of God," to readers to investigate. I, of course, prefer to say that during this sixth-century Dark Age time of suffering and woe, the demons Cold and Drought had mounted a successful attack. It is clear the world's climate in the Dark Ages was very unfavorable. Prior to the Dark Ages, there were several hundred years known as the *Roman Warm Period* or *Roman Climatic Optimum*. As implied, the era seems to have been relatively warm, perhaps nearly as warm as today. It may have spanned over 600 years—beginning about 250 BC and ending as late as AD 400. Certainly, during the time of Christ and the subsequent writing of the New Testament, the climate was favorable for population growth and the stability of the Roman Empire. Food was plentiful, and a surplus of labor permitted an unprecedented amount of construction of roads, viaducts, colosseums, urban areas, and so on. In the five to six thousand years prior to the rise of the Roman Empire, there were additional climate cycles alternating between *warm and wet* and *cold and dry*. These are less well-known and documented—with one prominent exception.

After the most recent Ice Age, the earth's climate warmed rapidly and global temperatures reached levels that were higher than today. This period is known variously as the *Climatic Optimum*, the *Hypisthermal*, or

ponderously, the *Post-Glacial Thermal Maximum*. Britain's Royal Meteorological Society published a book about this topic entitled *World Climate
from 8000 to 0 BC*. It addresses important questions such as what years
did this period cover and how warm was it. The introduction includes, for
example, the following question:

> Are we to accept that from 7500 BC to 700 BC or thereabouts,
> that much of Europe was warmer than today, and that the same
> could be said for eastern North America . . . Or should we agree
> to a period such as 5500 BC to 2000 BC?

Other questions debate how warm it was, with several ranges proposed
and debated. One rather awkward statement in the introduction states,
"the evidence from the vegetation supports a mean temperature lying between 1.5 degrees and 2 degrees C. above that of a period regarded as the
present." Sea level, the ultimate doom topic of the climate crazies, is also
investigated. This discussion of this subject begins with "during the last
glaciation sea level was about 100 meters lower than it is at present." More
to our interest, one contributor says, "What apparently now emerges is
that about 2000 BC the ocean level rose to about three meters above
the present height to which it gradually declined." Other proposed sea
levels and timelines are also supported. Plus, the higher sea levels were
not uniform around the entire globe. Be these outstanding questions as
they may, every study presents convincing evidence that by the end of the
Climatic Optimum, sea level had gradually risen to a maximum, which is
considerably higher than today—by as much as ten feet! This extremely
important topic is beyond the scope of this article. However, there is one
very important takeaway on the sea level question—the rise in sea level
because of the Climatic Optimum, to whatever maximum it reached,
was a process that took centuries, possibly even millennia. The climate
crazies incessantly claim that Miami, New Orleans, New York, etc., etc.,
will soon be flooded by several feet or even meters of water. Usually they
predict these untoward events will occur by about a week from Tues-
day. Admittedly, recently their timeline has lengthened somewhat. In the
1990s, dramatic and destructive rises in sea levels were *certain to happen*
within twenty years unless various draconian measures were mandated

and enforced. But none were. Thus, the tipping points, chain reactions, domino effects, and so on, should by now have made our coastal cities uninhabitable. Of late the climate crazies more frequently predict 2050 as the end of the world. A few now even admit it may take to the year 2100. Well, we should all take a deep breath and calm down. Yes, sea level is going to rise because of temperature increases. But this process is going to take centuries—not a couple, or even a few decades. In the year 2013, the National Geographic celebrated its 125th anniversary with a cover story showing the Statue of Liberty waist deep in water. Included in the special issue was a free poster showing how high the sea level would soon be throughout the entire world. Their dire predictions would make your blood run cold. Of course, National Geographic has a dismal record in these types of predictions. I have the magazine's June 1974 issue in my files. In it, National Geographic predicted (pp. 792–825) in a landmark analysis that the world's oil production would peak in 1995. By the year 2020, production would fall by more than half. By 2050, oil production was predicted to fall by 90 percent from the 1995 maximum. Other dire shortages of food and fresh water have been predicted from time to time by National Geographic, none of which have come about. All predictions about sea level rise, regardless of the source, should be viewed skeptically. The authors should be held to account by the press when their prognostications prove inaccurate. Oops, I forgot, the press can never be bothered to fact check anything.

The essential fact about the climate's oscillations over the past 10,000 years is that prior to the industrial age, all warm periods have been very good for humans. The original Climatic Optimum, the Roman Warm Period, and the MWP were all times of progress and prosperity. In contrast, famine and suffering marked the climate's cold periods. However, history may not repeat itself in the industrial age, now that the earth's population has grown to over eight billion. A warmer and wetter climate presents extremely complex issues. The truth is the climate's changes in the 21st Century will benefit some parts of the globe and be harmful to others.

I have previously described how the Chief Angel Warmth has done a wonderful job of warming Canada's temperatures since records begin in the 1800s. But, in fact, his partner Rain has been even more successful in defeating Drought in Canada. Earlier in this paper, I documented that the Great Drought of 1886–1895 was even more severe in central Canada than it was in the United States. I also showed there is much evidence that in Canada, this infamous drought probably began a year or two (or possibly even three) before it expanded south into the United States.

Therefore, this short section will be limited to precipitation in Canada, beginning in 1948. For context, it should be remembered that in the United States, the five driest consecutive years since the mid-1880s were 1952 through 1956, during which the annual precipitation averaged only 26.78 inches. To compare, the second driest five-year period in the United States was 1930 through 1934 when precipitation averaged 27.37 inches. During the past 50 years in the United States, there was only one five-year period which was drier than normal—1999 through 2003, which averaged 29.05 inches. The five-year drought of the 1950s in the United States peaked in 1956 when precipitation totaled only 25.38 inches. This total for 1956 was less precipitation than any year from 1917 to today. In 1956 it was so dry in Arizona (6.04 inches), New Mexico (6.58 inches), Kansas (15.34 inches), and parts of Utah and Oklahoma that it must have seemed like the end of the world. But finally the record drought of 1952–1956 in the United States lifted beginning in April 1957.

Why all this data about the 1952–1956 drought in the United States? Because it provides a necessary basis for comparing it to the much worse drought experienced by Canada. Serious drought began in Canada in 1948, the first year of its nationwide climate reporting. The precipitation records of various individual sites in Canada confirm this. Precipitation was much higher in all the Canadian sites I examined prior to 1948. As an example, the precipitation total for Winnipeg in 1948 was only 15.92 inches. Winnipeg's previous years totals were:

- 1947—21.96 inches

- 1946—16.35 inches

- 1945—22.73 inches

- 1944—24.33 inches
- 1941—24.60 inches

As in temperature, Canada's precipitation data is quite limited compared to the precision and volume of records for the United States. However, there is no doubt 1956 was by far the driest year in Canada since its national records began in 1948. Therefore, it is a virtual certainty that 1956 was the driest year in North America from 1917 through 2023, and perhaps even the driest year since 1910. I must admit no one knows about Mexico's annual precipitation totals before about the year 2000. Including anyone in Mexico! Canada's second driest year after 1947 was 1957, its third driest 1949, fourth was 1955, fifth was 1958, sixth 1948, and the seventh driest was 1950. The eleven years from 1948 to 1958 in Canada made up a continuous period of serious to record drought. Then, during each of the next eleven years, 1959 through 1969, Canada's precipitation remained below normal, varying from mild-to-moderate droughts.

But during the past fifty or more years, the good angel Rain has completely dominated Canada's climate, totally overpowering the evil demon Drought. Since 1970, there have only been eight years of below average precipitation in Canada but 46 years of above normal precipitation. In the year 2005, Canada received the most precipitation in the past 76 years, 2010 was the second highest, and 1998 the third greatest. The year 1978 was the only years of moderate to serious drought in Canada among the past 54 years. Climate change has been very kind to Canada since the 1800s, assuming the twin trends of increased temperature and precipitation are beneficial. The angels Warmth and Rain can be very proud of what they have accomplished in Canada and Alaska during the past century.

It is time to conclude what must have seemed like an endless recitation of numbers and statistics. Every quote is taken from either an official government document or current website. I have excluded no data which contradicts the twin premises of this analysis:

1. Precipitation in North America was much less in the 1800s than since 1900.

2. It was much colder (probably over the entire globe) but certainly in North America during the 1800s than since 1900.

I point out all data that does not show there was any unusual drought in California, Louisiana, and Florida during the 1800s.

I wish to leave you with two last examples. First, one of precipitation and second of temperature. Each concisely illustrates the two fundamental facts I have proven.

For precipitation, the following list gives the average annual precipitation for seven states, totaling 735,710 square miles in the West—Arizona, Colorado, Idaho, Montana, Nevada, Utah, and Wyoming—for each year 1886 through 1895. Also included are the ten-year precipitation averages for 1928 through 1937 and 1952 through 1961, which were the second and third driest ten-year periods for these states since 1886.

YEAR	SEVEN STATES AVG	10-YEAR AVG
1886	11.94	-------
1887	11.03	-------
1888	11.96	-------
1889	12.68	-------
1890	13.28	-------
1891	14.98	-------
1892	13.29	-------
1893	12.95	-------
1894	13.61	-------
1895	15.13	13.08
1928-37		14.54
1952-61		14.84

What does this data show? First, the ten-year cumulative average of 13.08 inches from 1886 through 1895 is MUCH LOWER than any other decade of drought seen since. The western third of Kansas (27,689 square miles) also received much less precipitation from 1886 through 1895 than in any other ten-year period and therefore it could have been included. But to keep the data *clean and simple,* I have limited to the seven states. Second, note the three driest years were the first three: 1886, 1887, and 1888, each averaging less than twelve inches. Third, note during the last two years, 1894 and 1895, the great drought is ending. Precipitation averaged 13.61 inches in 1894 and 1895 had 15.13 inches, the highest precipitation of the ten extremely dry years. The average precipitation in 1896, (not included in the table above) was 17.15 inches and in 1897, the seven states averaged 17.57 inches. Unfortunately, precipitation data for these states for years prior to 1886 is unavailable. But if precipitation in 1885 was less than 1895, the long-term average would be even less. And if precipitation in 1884 was less than in 1894, it would be still less, and so on.

The above data proves beyond any doubt that the drought in the western United States (not to mention the substantial evidence I provided of even greater drought in central Canada during this era) was much worse in 1886 through 1895 than anything experienced since then. And common sense would admit the substantial likelihood that it was even worse if precipitation data for 1883, 1884, 1885, etc. were available. Here are a few examples:

- Helena, MT
  - 1885—10.99 inches
  - 1886—12.63 inches
- Havre, MT
  - 1885—8.37 inches
  - 1886—11.48 inches

- Crow Agency, MT
  - 1885—9.34 inches
  - 1886—13.25 inches
- Miles City, MT
  - 1885—10.28 inches
  - 1886—13.14 inches

The much lower precipitation amounts received in 1885 provide evidence that the great drought of 1886–1895 probably began before 1886 in the north and expanded south in subsequent years.

For temperature, please recall that for the 130-year period of record, 1895 through 2024, the temperature in the contiguous 48 states has increased at a rate of 1.72 degrees per century. Therefore, isn't it curious, even noteworthy, that the rate of increase in the period 1895 through 1955 (see the official NOAA graph below) was higher, at 1.85 degrees per century? Have you ever heard the climate cultists say that temperatures in the first part of the official period of record were increasing at a faster rate than during the period as a whole? Of course not! They hate this fact and are loath to admit it! The climate crazies want everyone to think that temperature increases are only very recent. But the fact is warmer temperatures are a trend which is firmly supported by all data for as far back as the first instrument records. I did not *cherry pick* the period 1895 through 1955. Obviously, I would begin the example with 1895, the first year available, and then select a later year as the end. I chose 1955 as the end just because it is a round number. The 61 years, 1895 through 1955, meet the scientific criteria of comparing two periods of at least 30 years. Actually, the temperature increase would have been even greater if I had ended my example a year earlier, with 1954.

Consider these facts, the average temperature in the CONUS in the 30 years 1895 through 1924 was 51.50°. The average temperature in the next 30 years, 1925 through 1954, was 52.26° or 0.76 degrees warmer.

I am taking the liberty of rounding this increase down to 0.75 degrees. Now please recall that in my analysis of the annual temperature of 40 *first order* climate stations, I found that the average annual temperature in the 20-year period 1895 through 1914 was 0.532 degrees warmer than the average annual temperature of the 40 stations in the previous 20-years 1875 through 1894. I am also rounding this increase down to 0.50 degrees. An increase of 0.50 degrees over twenty years is at the same annual rate as 0.75 degrees over 30 years. Thus, I believe the data supports the conclusion that the temperature in the CONUS was increasing at a rate of about 0.025 degrees. annually from 1875 through 1954. Of course, I maintain (and believe I have proven) that temperatures in North America had been increasing for at least several decades prior to 1875. However, I concede insufficient data exists to accurately calculate the annual rate of increase before 1875.

If, therefore, the temperature was increasing at a rate of 0.75 degrees over 30 years, temperature would have averaged 53.0° in the period 1955 through 1984 (52.25° plus 0.75) the average temperature in the next 30 years, 1985 through 2014 would have been 53.75°. (53.0° plus 0.75). Finally, during the past nine years, 2015 through 2023, the average temperature would have increased an additional 0.225 degrees (0.025 times nine) and the annual average temperature in the most recent 30 years, 1994 through 2023 would have been 53.975° (53.75° plus 0.225). There is no flaw in the math, if one agrees that by 1954 the rate of temperature increase in the CONUS had been established at about 0.025 degrees per year. The estimated increase of 0.025 degrees per year is, in fact, a little conservative, given that I rounded down the initial rates slightly.

What has been the actual temperature increase in the CONUS, compared to the temperature increase I predicted based on the record from 1875 through 1954? The average annual temperature in the CONUS during the most recent 30 years, 1994 through 2023, is 53.454°. This is 0.521 degrees below the average I predicted of 53.975°. In summary, the temperature in the CONUS over the past 30 years has averaged a over 0.50 degrees *cooler* than if they had continued to increase at 0.025 degree per year since 1954.

What if I used more recent periods of less than 30 years? I provide the following examples, with the proviso that using shorter periods when discussing climate change is less reliable, and the shorter the periods, the less reliable. CONUS temperature in the most recent ten years, 2014 through 2023 averaged 53.928°, which is nearly as warm as the predicted 53.975° average for the past 30 years. How about the most recent five years? CONUS temperature averaged 53.870 in the most recent five years, 2019 through 2023, which is slightly *below* the ten-year average. This is because the initial five years, 2014 through 2018, were warmer, averaging 53.985° than the second five years, 2019 through 2023. How many times have you heard the climate crazies point out that on average CONUS temperature during the 2019 through 2023 years were actually *slightly cooler* than the previous five years? Never, of course!

The rate of temperature increase is very important in the debate over the anthropogenic causes of climate change. How much of the increase in temperature, whether in the cold or warm months, or in the north or south of the continent, or in the early or later part of the period for which there is accurate instrument data is because of human activity? According to the climate cultists ALL the increase in temperature has been, and will continue to be caused by humans. But as for the cause of the increase in precipitation, which has been much greater than temperature, they remain silent. They can't even consider, much less accept, that human activity might cause anything beneficial. So they remain mum on why there has been a wonderfully beneficial increase in precipitation. As far as their rigid attitude toward the cause of the increase in temperature, I am reminded of Mark Twain's famous saying, "Faith is the ability to believe what you know ain't so."

Science cannot say how much of the increase in temperature is because of either natural or anthropogenic causes. But we should be broad-minded enough to consider all possibilities. Remember, there is a case, not at all far-fetched, that the Little Ice Age began around the year 1200 and that its coldest time was about 500 years later, around the year 1700. If the great *cool down* of the Little Ice Age took about five centuries, is it not even remotely possible that the subsequent warm-up would also last around 500 years? If so, then the natural warming cycle would last from about 1700 to about the year 2200. Even if the natural warming is for only 400 years, temperature would increase until around the year 2100. I am sure that most climate cultists would like to wring my neck for suggesting this as a scenario. But only the most contrived, biased, and intellectually indefensible position is that *all* the *natural warming* rebound from the Little Ice Age was completed at some time in the past (pray tell us by what exact year?) and that therefore *all* the increase in temperature since said year was because of human activity.

A basic underlying fact is that from 1875 (and perhaps before) to about 1955, the temperature in the CONUS increased at a rate of about 0.025 degrees per year. This 75 to 80-year period is long enough to establish approximately 0.025 degrees per year as a normal rate of temperature increase in the CONUS coming out of the Little Ice Age. If the rate of increase since 1955 exceeds 0.025 degrees per year by a substantial amount, it would be logical to conclude the increased rate, or most of it, is due to human activity.

Regardless of the cause(s) of the climate's changes since the inception of instrument records, the critical question remains if the changes have been (and are) harmful or beneficial. The residents of each state, or perhaps even each climate division, should be allowed to reach their own conclusions without outside interference. In some states, Nebraska, for example, the changes seen in Climate Division 1, Panhandle, are quite different that those recorded in Climate Division 9, Southeast. But for a simple example, I will use my home state of South Dakota as the prime case. The changes seen in each of its nine climate divisions vary somewhat, but are basically quite similar.

I will begin with precipitation since I assert it is the climate's most important factor. It certainly is in South Dakota! During the past 130 years, 1895 through 2024, precipitation in South Dakota averaged 19.32 inches per year. It is known that prior to 1895 precipitation in South Dakota averaged considerably less than 19.32 inches. But still today, South Dakota has a very dry climate. Born in 1947, I grew up hearing on the radio or reading in the newspaper that we were "desperate for rain," or that we were "crying for rain" or even "dying for rain." I also heard these comments from my friends and neighbors and parents and older siblings. I never once heard that we'd had too much rain, or that we wished it would stop raining. Of course, I know this inevitably happened from time to time, at least on a local scale.

The fundamental problem in South Dakota has always been drought. It is plagued with extended dry spells that go on for years and sometimes even decades. Ann Marie Lowe, in her book *Dust Bowl Diary,* said that 1927 was "the last good year" in North Dakota. The same might well be said for South Dakota because it received 22.74 inches in 1927, which was then the seventh highest annual amount on record. But as in North Dakota, the nation's Great Drought of the 1930s began two years earlier in South Dakota. Only 17.16 inches were received in 1928. Then the drought continued for over three decades! In the 34 years, 1928 through 1961, South Dakota averaged only 17.68 inches per year. It was a long dreary 34 years of less than adequate precipitation. Thankfully, the Lord provided some relief during the World War II years when the United States was helping to feed the free world. I have been told that my maternal grandfather Leon DeWitt Howard of Blunt, born in 1870, virtually worked himself to death during the war years repairing farm equipment, improvising with determination, ingenuity, and skill because there were no spare parts nor any men to help with his repair business. A complete invalid during his final years, grandpa died in 1950. Other than the short miraculous reprieve of manna from heaven in the early 1940s, 1928 through 1961, saw 34 years of hardship and deprivation. Then in 1962, precipitation increased in South Dakota and the trend has been upward, with only minor interruptions, for the past 60 or more years.

As proof of this, during the most recent 32 years, 1993 through 2024, precipitation in South Dakota has averaged 21.05 inches. The economy has been transformed—much for the better. No longer do we hear gallows humor such as,

"What's the difference between a crow and a farmer?"
"A crow can make a deposit on a tractor!"

The difference between decades of drought when precipitation averaged 17.68 inches and recent decades, which average 21.05 inches, is simple—poverty vs. prosperity.

Considering temperature, during the past 130 years, South Dakota's annual temperature has averaged 44.75°, a very cold climate. Again, it is known that South Dakota's climate was considerably colder prior to 1895. It has seen incredible cold in the past. In 1936 and again in 1937, the temperature averaged below zero for an entire month. The coldest month was February 1936, which averaged minus 5.2°. South Dakota frequently has the five-month winter described earlier when the temperature drops below freezing in November and stays below 32° until April. The year I graduated from high school, November averaged 30.2° Then four months of miserable cold followed and in March 1965 it still averaged only 19.2°!

The changing climate means that South Dakota has been getting warmer, having warmed at a rate of 2.0 degrees per century since 1895, slightly faster than the 48-state average of 1.72 degrees. We'd wish for more warming but we'll take what we can get! Fortunately, most of the warming has occurred in the colder months. December has warmed at 2.4 degrees per century, January at an acceptable rate of 3.9 degrees, February even faster at 4.9 degrees and March, by which time people are really sick of the cold, has warmed at 4.0 degrees per century. You may expect that the warming has resulted in unpleasantly warm summers, since the Great Plains can get amazingly hot. In a word, No! The three warmest months in South Dakota have been July 1936 which averaged 83.3°, July 2012 with 78.7°, and July 1935 averaging 78.5° During the past 32 years, 1993 through 2024, during which precipitation averaged over 21 inches, there have been only three summer months of unusually warm temperature in South Dakota, the most recent was July 2012.

So, if given a choice, which would you rather have? Precipitation averaging less than 18 inches or the present annual average of over 21 inches. If you had to choose between cold as hell for five consecutive winter months or a long-term trend toward much milder winters, which would it be? I believe that the vast majority of residents in South Dakota would say that the changes in the climate have been highly beneficial and they would hope and pray the trends seen in recent decades continue.

There would, of course, be a minority who would claim that the extended droughts and extreme cold seen back in "the good old days" were conditions of a better climate. These poor folks are to be pitied. They've been infected by the dreaded *Woke Mind Virus*. It has seized control of their brains and removed their ability to reason! It's very sad when this happens—it's a modern-day malady often seen among pot smokers and opioid addicts, whose thinking is muddled on many topics.

The same metrics South Dakotans would apply can, of course, be used in every state. North Dakotans would be even more likely to say that the changes in its climate since it entered the union have been the greatest thing since the Homestead Act. But how about Arkansas, or Colorado, or Ohio? I don't presume to speculate. The essential fact is the specific changes seen in each state are extremely important. As a general idea, the term *climate change* seems to imply danger and probably harm. However, once people look at their state's specific changes and trends closely, the residents of Iowa, Tennessee, and many others just might well say, "What's not to like?"

To continue to dominate the subject, and maintain their Orwellian hold over the minds of the masses, the climate crazies must preserve several carefully crafted fictions.

First, they must deny that in the past the climate was adverse and frankly horrible. Or, if they can't deny it, they must studiously continue to ignore the past. They must ensure it is not investigated, documented, and compared to today. Droughts of the 1800s, which in some cases persisted for decades, can't be acknowledged or even mentioned. Nor can the past's intense extreme and long-lasting cold be recognized as dangerous, harmful, costly, and even deadly.

Second, the climate cultists must prevent the public from examining and learning about the detailed climate changes in their state or area. This would allow them to form educated opinions on whether the trends are harmful or beneficial. The last thing they want is for the residents of Michigan's Upper Peninsula to learn the detailed facts and contemplate what the changes mean for their society, culture, and economy. Michigan's Climate Division 1 has recorded months in the distant past when temperature averaged below zero. The coldest month was January 1912, which averaged minus 6.2°. But January in Division 1 has been warming at a rate of 3.3 degrees per century and (believe it or not) February has been warming at 5.0 degrees per century! Since 1895, the division's precipitation has increased at a rapid rate of 2.34 inches per century, resulting in the division's long-term precipitation average increasing to 31.33 inches per year. It would cause untold difficulties to the climate crazies' cause if the people of Marquette, Michigan, Sioux City, Iowa or a hundred other locations really knew what has happened to their climate since the 1800s. The climate crazies must maintain the fiction that whatever the changes are—they are bad! Therefore, people needn't bother to learn the specifics of what their area's exact changes have been. Just move along folks . . . there's nothing to see here!

I have previously stated that the changes in the climate have been favorable to agriculture and the production of food. I now provide data which supports this. The government has tracked the production of various crops and commodities since 1866. The Department of Agriculture published its most recent comprehensive statistical report (368 pages) in April 2024. It documents every major crop produced in the United States, with some data beginning in 1866. The three primary crops in the United States since the end of World War II have been the staple cereal grains of corn and wheat, plus soybeans, "the miracle crop with a thousand uses." Below are the production totals in thousands of bushels for each crop for the ten years 1950 through 1959, compared to the totals for the most recent ten years, 2014 through 2023. I selected the 1950s because war did not affect production during that decade.

U.S. Historical Crop Production:
1950s vs. most recent ten years: 2014–2023.

CORN		WHEAT		SOYBEANS	
1950	2,764,071	1950	1,019,344	1950	299,249
1951	2,628,937	1951	988,161	1951	283,777
1952	2,980,793	1952	1,306,440	1952	298,839
1953	2,881,801	1953	1,173,071	1953	269,169
1954	2,707,913	1954	983,900	1954	341,075
1955	2,872,959	1955	937,094	1955	373,682
1956	3,075,336	1956	1,005,397	1956	449,251
1957	3,045,355	1957	955,740	1957	483,425
1958	3,356,205	1958	1,457,435	1958	580,260
1959	3,824,598	1959	1,117,735	1959	532,899
TOTAL	30,137,968	TOTAL	10,944,317	TOTAL	3,911,626
2014	14,217,292	2014	2,026,310	2014	3,928,070
2015	13,601,984	2015	2,061,939	2015	3,926,779
2016	15,148,038	2016	2,308,663	2016	4,296,496
2017	14,609,407	2017	1,740,910	2017	4,411,633
2018	14,321,674	2018	1,885,361	2018	4,428,150
2019	13,568,306	2019	1,932,017	2019	3,551,070
2020	14,086,699	2020	1,819,673	2020	4,216,302
2021	15,017,788	2021	1,646,254	2021	4,464,492
2022	13,650,531	2022	1,649,713	2022	4,270,381
2023	15,341,595	2023	1,811,977	2023	4,164,677
TOTAL	143,563,314	TOTAL	18,882,817	TOTAL	41,658,050

Source: USDA Agricultural Statistics Service Report No. 2157-8990, April 2024.

The above data requires a brief explanation because of the production of wheat increased by *only* 73 percent since the 1950s, compared to a 364 percent increase in corn and a 965 percent increase in the production of soybeans. Wheat production in the United States peaked in 1981 at 2,785,357,000 bushels. But because of the scientific work of Norman Borlaug, the only plant breeder ever to win the Nobel Prize, the world now has a large surplus of wheat. Wheat is now grown and exported in gigantic amounts by Russia, Ukraine, Canada, Argentina, Australia, and even India. The price of wheat on the world market has remained low compared to oil and just about everything else. Wheat is not a priority for the United States because export demand is meager and profits are minimal. The climate of North America would support a gigantic increase in the production of wheat any time the market improves and farmers decide to plant more acres.

There will be those who object to this summary. They will claim that the 1950s is a poor period to compare to today, etc. I simply challenge the predictable nay sayers to read the entire 368-page report. On page 205, they will find, for example, that the production of rice in the United States increased from 38,820 cwt. in 1950 to 218,291 cwt. in 2023. No matter what base period is chosen, the record shows a significant increase in production in every crop or commodity.

Taken in their entirety, United States agricultural production statistics show tremendous increases in every crop and commodity the industry has produced. This could only be accomplished with a favorable climate. The increase in precipitation combined with much longer growing seasons has had the result every farmer would naturally expect. Record crops! Not even the most neurotic climate cultist can deny that the modern North American climate has led to record harvests.

Lenin supposedly said that journalists could be harnessed to serve as "useful idiots." They were easily controlled and manipulated to promote and advance the revolution's propaganda. The last challenge of the climate cultists is to maintain control of the press. In the *post-truth* era, this isn't as difficult as is sounds. The media are incurious, indolent, and has no sense of history. They're content to be spoon fed. But there is still the possibility that a reporter, editor, or even an elected official may look at the facts and have the courage to speak out. To be sure, a voice crying in the wilderness risks being *canceled* by the woke mob. Therefore, only time will tell if the horrible climate of the 1800s, as well as the beneficial effects of the recent changes, ever become known and considered in a rational and dispassionate way.

Notes on Sources

I will not repeat the various books and articles mentioned or cited in the text. Those given below are the main additional reference sources used for temperature and precipitation data; many being essential for studying the climate of North America prior to 1900.

The single best volume about climate in the United States is *Climate and Man*, 1,248 pages, published by the federal government in 1941; House Document 27, 77th Congress, 1st Session. This timeless, extremely comprehensive book was republished twenty years later by Gale Research Company. This is one of the primary sources of annual precipitation (and other data) for each state and the entire nation, beginning in 1886 and extending through 1938.

Since 1852 the Smithsonian Institution has published a Volume of Meteorological Tables. The sixth revised edition, by Robert J. List, 527 pages, issued August 1971, is an invaluable reference. It containing 173 reference tables on scientific weather-related topics.

Second in importance is the series *World Weather Records*. The Smithsonian Institution published the first three volumes of this massive and highly respected series. These contain weather and climate data and analysis for sites around the globe from the 1700s through 1940. In 1941, the United States Department of Commerce took over this series, and has published one volume per decade since the 1950s.

A massive mine of data is contained in the series *Climatic Summary of the United States*, a series of four volumes published by the government from 1932 through 1934. Totaling 3,047 pages, climate data from every known site, presented for the nation by 106 sections (Section 1 is Western Washington, etc.) from inception through 1930 can be found therein. There is no need to find a paper copy in a library because each volume can easily be called up on the internet.

A superior and easy-to-use internet source is the Climate at a Glance site run by NOAA. Data beginning in January 1895, by month, season, and year, is readily available for state, 344 climate divisions, regions, and national totals. The information is presented using both tables and graphs. This is indeed unique and everyone interested in the climate should know how to use this website. As an example, one can find that Arizona Climate Division 5 (Southwest, 10,013 Square Miles) received only 0.87 inches of precipitation in 1956. In contrast, Louisiana Climate Division 9 (Southeast, 6,165 Square Miles) received 92.89 inches of precipitation in 1991, over 100 times as much. But a major weakness of this website is that it does not have any data prior to 1895. And as I have shown, knowledge of North America's climate prior to 1895 is essential.

Two additional very extensive and relevant publications by the federal government are *Crop Yields and Weather* published jointly by the Department of Agriculture and the Department of Commerce in February 1942 and *Fluctuations in Crops and Weather 1866—1948*, published in June 1951 by the Department of Agriculture. Both contain massive amounts of data on climate statistics and agricultural output by state, month, year, type of crop and so on. The second of the two studies cited is the most complete. Remarkably, each of these seminal works shows that cold and dry conditions result in poor crops and warm and wet weather lead to much larger harvests. Isn't this extremely odd? According to the hollow reasoning of climate crazies, a warmer climate with longer growing seasons and plentiful rainfall should cause crop failures and even famine. But of course, the exact opposite has always been true, as both these volumes prove decisively.

A gigantic encyclopedic source published by the Department of Agriculture in 1936 is the *Atlas of American Agriculture: Physical Basis Including Land Relief, Climate, Soils and Natural Vegetation*. This book measures 24 by 36 inches and weighs eight pounds. A very rare edition, it contains beautiful and unique full-color maps of temperature, precipitation, soil types and topography. Today, it is doubtful the government would even attempt to produce such an amazing and comprehensive volume.

I have also consulted and recommend the *Monthly Weather Review*. This is the government's scientific journal, which was started in the 1870s. It goes much beyond its title and has articles on weather and climate events and forecasting from both the United States and around the world. Similar to the monthly reports, but containing yearly summary data and analysis are the annual reports of the Weather Bureau and its predecessors, published since 1872. These annual reports have had several titles over the years depending on whether the Department of Agriculture or the Department of Commerce published them. Until 1935, they were issued as *Report of the Chief of the Weather Bureau*. After that, they are called the *United States Meteorological Yearbook*. Sadly, they were discontinued in 1949, except for a poorly done final summary report published in 1952. All the annual reports can be read and downloaded from the internet.

A little-known but very important document is the report *The Future of the Great Plains*, published in December 1936 and transmitted to the Congress for its consideration by President Franklin Roosevelt in February 1937. President Roosevelt commissioned this report and appointed a Select Committee of experts to write it. Why was this report needed? Because the climate of the Great Plains had been a disaster, both in the 1930s and as I have documented earlier. The report documents and confirms this. It was to address the long running tragedy and serve as a basis for drafting legislation to provide relief and solutions. But nothing was ever done. This high-profile report which made headlines when it was issued is now long forgotten. Fortunately, the whole topic is now moot, as conditions on the Great Plains have improved. In truth, the plains have been transformed dramatically for the better because of climate change.

Today, contrary to the portrayals of the climate cultists, the Great Plains are prosperous and no longer need any special attention or help.

Two additional essential but seldom consulted federal reports which I used are the *Report on the Climate of Arizona with Particular Reference to Rainfall and Water Storage in the Arid Region*, House of Representatives, 51st Congress, 2nd Session, 105 pages, Government Printing Office, 1891, and *Climate of Nebraska, Particularly in Reference to the Temperature and Rain-fall and Their Influence Upon the Agricultural Interests of the State*, United States Senate, 51st Congress, 1st Session, 172 pages, Government Printing Office, 1890. These studies extended much beyond the boundaries of the two states listed in their titles. Together they encompass almost all the western United States, and contain virtually all temperature and precipitation data from every site through the dates of their printing. These reports were commissioned by Congress because the climate in the West was extremely different from the settled parts of the country. The data gathered fully revealed the extent of these differences. Thus, both the government and potential future inhabitants were warned of the challenges inherent in a cold and arid climate.

A better known and more frequently cited document is John Wesley Powell's famous *Report on the Land of the Arid Region of the United States*, 45th Congress, 2nd Session, 202 pages, plus maps, published in final form by the Senate in March 1879. Harvard University reprinted this landmark work in 1962, with Wallace Stegner as editor. Therefore, it is much more readily available than the two reports mentioned above. Powell was the Director of the United States Geographical and Geological Survey and this was by far the most thorough and scientific examination of the West the government had done up to that year. The West is summarized as "a semi-desert with a desert heart." This report was factual but highly controversial, at least then. To be blunt, Powell said the West was extremely dry. Every exploration, beginning with Colonel Stephen Long's mission in the 1820s, found this to be so. However, because of the changing climate, there has been a substantial increase in precipitation since the 1800s, which has dramatically reduced the size of the West's semi-desert and its arid heart.

Two more early but very comprehensive and useful reports by the Weather Bureau are the *Temperature Departures, Monthly and Annual in the United States January 1873 to June 1909, Inclusive* (also known as *Bulletin U*), published in 1911 and *Climatology of the United States* (also known as *Bulletin Q*) by Alfred Judson Henry, published in 1906. *Bulletin U* has 474 separate charts, one for each month and one for each year. These are maps of the contiguous 48 states and clearly illustrate episodes of extreme cold I referenced in the text. The November 1880 map, for example, shows a gigantic area in the center of the country where the temperature was 10, 12, 14, and finally 16 degrees below normal. The subsequent map for December 1880 also shows an area as much as 16 degrees below normal. The extreme departures from normal temperatures continued in the early months of 1881. January had areas over ten degrees below normal, February 1881 again had areas 16 degrees below normal, and both March and April 1881 contained areas eight degrees below normal. November 1880 through April 1881 was a six-month winter the likes of which have not been approached since the 1800s. The report documents that the two coldest consecutive months were January and February 1875. Both months had extensive areas of the country where the temperature was at least 16 degrees below normal.

Bulletin Q is a gigantic report, 1,012 pages, which summarizes all the climate data gathered in the United States from the early 1800s through December 31, 1903. It has maps and tables for precipitation and temperature for every season, state, and region. Each state is divided into sections and further detailed reports are provided for each climate station. The report notes, for example, that in my home state of South Dakota, the station in Aberdeen, Brown County, the temperature ranged from minus 46° in February 1899 to a high of 111° a year later in August 1900. The range from coldest to hottest temperature was an amazing 157° The climate of the Great Plains in the old days definitely wasn't suited to sissies! Of course, it's much nicer in the Great Plains now due to climate change.

A very helpful source for Canada's climate is the internet publication entitled *Climate Trends and Variations Bulletin*. Quarterly issues are published for each season, followed by an annual summary report. This source is limited in that Canada's comprehensive national climate data begins in January 1948. Prior to 1948, Canada's less comprehensive climate data is available for individual cities and sites, beginning with Toronto in 1841. This data can be found on the website Environment Canada. Much can also be found in the *World Weather Records* series.

I am the proud owner of perhaps the rarest and most valuable book ever published on the climate of North America. It is the *Climatology of the United States and of the Temperate Latitudes of the North American Continent* by Loren Blodget, 536 pages, with many foldout maps and charts. Published by J. P. Lippincott and Co., Philadelphia, June, 1857. Mine is a copy in fine condition. It contains much unique data on the climate and conditions in North America prior to 1850. Blodget's data and analysis have never been fully reproduced in any other volume since 1857. I keep this highly prized possession under lock and key in a fireproof file cabinet.

I also have the reports of Zebulon Pike's, 1806-1807, and Major Stephen Long's 1819-1820, expeditions. Without exception, they concluded the West was extremely dry. Pike famously said, "The vast plains of the Western Hemisphere may become in time equally celebrated as the sandy deserts of Africa." Long was even more somber in his report concluding, "The traveller [*sic*] who shall at any time have traversed its (the West's) desolate sands, will, we think, join us in the wish that the region may forever remain the unmolested haunt of the native hunter, the bison, and the jackall [*sic*]."

Congress published the report by Stephen Long and the famous botanist Dr. Edwin James, the lead scientist accompanying the expedition in 1823. It was reprinted and analyzed in the book *From Pittsburgh to the Rocky Mountains—Major Stephen Long's Expedition 1819-1820*, 410 pages, 1988, Fulcrum Books, Golden, Colorado. The editors closely considered Long's famous description of the lands they explored as "The Great American Desert" and frankly agreed saying, "it is difficult to see how Long and James could have come to any other conclusion regarding the usefulness of the area . . . they found it impossible to believe that civilization as they knew it could survive and survive in that inhospitable territory. Better to leave it to the wild animals and the Indians, they thought, no sensible person would choose to make a life in that country." Given what we now know about how dry it was in the West in the 1800s, the report's findings seem obvious and uncontroversial.

But Pike, Long, and James were certainly not the first to reach these conclusions. Every explorer beginning with Coronado said essentially the same thing. Coronado's chronicles of his expedition, 1540–1542, through what is now Arizona, New Mexico, Texas, Oklahoma, and as far north as what is now Dodge City, Kansas spoke of the "great arid desert through which they travelled." A few years ago, a trendy and appealing theory appeared in the media. It espoused the idea that precipitation in the West was greater in the 1600s, or maybe it was in the 1700s. Details and specifics were lacking. Full of conjecture, the new theory was completely without evidence. It made headlines in *USA Today* and other publications of similar ilk. But the fact is this nonsense is completely contradicted by the accounts of everyone since 1540 who actually set foot in the West.

It is worth noting the collapse of the Ancestral Puebloan culture, with 30,000 inhabitants, in Mesa Verde and many other similar sites in Colorado, New Mexico, and Arizona is primarily attributed to prolonged drought. There is no sign of violence or disease among the human remains or other archaeological evidence. Extreme drought is the only probable cause of the mass migrations. Many investigations and studies have confirmed this. Perhaps those who try to claim the American West had higher precipitation in the 1700s (or whenever) have it confused with Shangri-La.

A nearly unique book which verifies the precipitation data found elsewhere is *Drought: Its Causes and Effects* by Ivan Ray Tannehill, 264 pages, published by Princeton University Press in 1947. It has comprehensive tables and maps of precipitation by state, the three then used climate divisions (Wester, Middle, and Eastern) and the nation, year-by-year, for the 59-year period 1886 through 1945. Dr. Tannehill seems to be the only scholar who has authored a volume exclusively dedicated to the study of drought. His research included a thorough examination of drought in the 1800s to the extent possible for years prior to 1886. He concluded that the year 1860 was probably the driest year ever seen up to 1945 in North America.

A rather foundational document on the whole climate change topic is a report titled *RESTORING THE QUALITY OF OUR ENVIRONMENT*, written by the Environmental Pollution Panel of the President's Science Advisory Committee. This report was released to the public by President Lyndon Johnson on November 5, 1965. The report considered very many environmental problems, including soil pollution, the polluting effects of detergents, mining wastes, pesticides, water quality, and many others. The Superintendent of Documents printed the whole thing, over 300 pages, and offered for sale for $1.25. Well, believe it or not, one of the subpanel reports was entitled *Atmospheric Carbon Dioxide*. So, as far back as 1965, the federal government had labeled carbon dioxide in the atmosphere as a pollutant. Never mind, of course, that CO_2 is essential for plant photosynthesis and is a critically important *greenhouse gas*. Without the *greenhouse effect*, the earth since its creation would have been locked in a perpetual ice age. Within the 300-page document, the report of the CO_2 subpanel is Appendix Y4. The appendix comprises 21 pages and, perhaps surprisingly; it is extremely good! It is measured, well-reasoned, under-stated, and completely lacks the frenzied tone and apocalyptic hysteria that characterizes anything and everything produced by today's climate cultists. At the end of this Appendix is a list of 35 references, including articles, books, even "Letters to the Editor" in newspapers about carbon dioxide, whether it is found in the atmosphere, oceans, vegetation, and even the soil and rocks. These important references were published be-tween 1938 and the first half of 1965.

On September 17, 1969, Daniel Patrick Moynihan, then President Rich-ard Nixon's Assistant for Domestic Policy, distributed a memorandum warning about the danger of increases in atmospheric carbon dioxide. Since then, this memorandum has received both praise and condemna-tion. It can easily be read and downloaded on the internet. Less than two pages long, he begins by alerting his readers to "apocalyptic change" in the future. The heart of the memo is found in the second paragraph when he says, "It is now pretty clearly agreed that the CO_2 content will rise 25% by 2000. This could increase the average temperature near the earth's surface by 7 degrees Fahrenheit and raise sea level by ten feet. Goodbye, New York. Goodbye Washington, for that matter." Sadly, this silly rubbish means that the climate crazies revere and pay homage to the memory of Moynihan. To them, he is a genuine hero. But in fact, he was the first member of the WSNCC (Worldwide Society of Neurotic Climate Cultists). The trouble is, nothing about the memo was accurate—not even close. First, in 1969 there was no "pretty clear agreement" on future CO_2 rise. And of course, neither the dramatic temperature increases nor the sea level inundations of New York City (his home) or any other cities came about. The average temperature of the 48 contiguous states in the 30 years 1940 through 1969 was 51.97°. The average CONUS temperature in the next 30 years, 1970 through 1999, was 52.27°. The temperature increase was not 7 degrees, but 0.3 degrees Moynihan was off by only 96 percent. And the sea level rise from 1970 to 2000 was not 10 feet, nor was it even ten inches, it was only a few centimeters. Moynihan died in 2003. Thankfully, he didn't need to say goodbye to New York City—it had remained high and dry and still is.

I also referenced and recommend to any reader several general books on weather and climate, perhaps beginning with *The American Weather Book*, 1982, by David M. Ludlum. In it Ludlum chronicled weather events for each day of the year since the 1630s and summarizes instrument data beginning in South Carolina in 1737 and Massachusetts in 1742. The climate cultists would probably destroy all known copies of this book if they could, since it reveals how adverse and frankly terrible the climate of North America was prior to the 20th Century. *Climatic Change—Evidence, Causes, and Effects*, Harlow Shapley, Editor, published by Harvard University Press, is one of the pioneering studies on the subject. Interestingly, it was published in 1953 (!) and was an alternate selection of the Book of the Month Club. It proves that *climate change* is not at all new or just a recently discovered topic, as the media often claims. It is well known that the climate has been changing since the earliest instrument records. The difference is that until about 30 years ago, the warming climate, coupled with increased precipitation, was, for good reason, considered being highly favorable trends.

Also of great interest is *Times of Feast, Times of Famine—A History of Climate Since the Year 1000*, 426 pages, 1971, by Professor Emmanuel Le Roy Ladurie of the University of Paris. The professor tracks the advances and retreats of glaciers, plentiful and poor crop harvests, the rise and decline of disease and everything else related to or a consequence of the climate. Some of his data begins as early as the year AD 820. The book is superior, but you needn't bother reading it. It can be well summarized in just one sentence: *Times of feast were warm and times of famine were cold.*

Last, I recommend those who are interested in the climate to read any of the several major surveys on the subject. I would begin with *Climate History and the Modern World*, 2nd Edition, Routledge, London and New York, by H. H. Lamb. Lamb is one of the most highly respected scientists in this discipline. He writes not to promote an agenda or narrative (unlike many others), but simply documents the climate throughout history, together with the effects it had on the world.

About the Author

Mr. Hyde has written books and articles on the history of arms limitation, the demographic decline of Western Civilization, consequences of the "birth dearth" in the Great Plains and other history-related topics. His previous book on climate, "Climate Change - A Brief History of the Last 50 Million Years," was published by Legacy Book Publishing in 2015. Hyde and his late wife Robin served as Peace Corps Volunteers in Bulgaria. He has appeared on the ABC News program Nightline and was interviewed on National Public Radio's "Weekend Edition." Hyde joined the Rotary in 2000 and has lived in DeLand, Florida since October 2007.

www.ingramcontent.com/pod-product-compliance
Lightning Source LLC
Chambersburg PA
CBHW052113090426

42741CB00009B/1789